Illinois
NOTARY PRIMER

The NNA's Handbook for Illinois Notaries

Thirteenth Edition

Published by:

National Notary Association
9350 De Soto Avenue
Chatsworth, CA 91311-4926
Telephone: (800) 876-6827
Fax: (818) 700-0920
Website: NationalNotary.org
Email: nna@NationalNotary.org

The information in this *Primer* is correct and current at the
time of its publication although new laws, regulations and
rulings may subsequently affect the validity of certain sections.
This information is provided to aid comprehension of state
Notary Public requirements and should not be construed as
legal advice. Please consult an attorney for inquiries relating to
legal matters.

Thirteenth Edition ©2024
First Edition ©2001

ISBN: 978-1-59767-332-7

Table of Contents

Have a Tough Notary Question?

If you were a National Notary Association member, you could get the answer to that difficult question. Join the NNA® and your membership includes access to the NNA® Hotline* and live Notary experts providing the latest Notary information regarding laws, rules and regulations.

Hours

Monday – Friday	5:00 a.m.–6:30 p.m. (PT)
Saturday	5:00 a.m.–5:00 p.m. (PT)

NNA® Hotline Toll-Free Phone Number: 1-888-876-0827

After hours you can leave a message or email our experts at Hotline@NationalNotary.org and they will respond the next business day.

*Access to the NNA® Hotline is for National Notary Association members and NNA® Hotline subscribers only. Call and become a member today.

Introduction

The National Notary Association commends you on your interest in Illinois Notary law. Purchasing the *Illinois Notary Primer* identifies you as a conscientious professional who takes your official responsibilities seriously.

In few fields is the expression "more to it than meets the eye" truer than in Notary law. What often appears on the surface to be a simple procedure may, in fact, have important legal considerations.

The purpose of the *Illinois Notary Primer* is to provide you with a resource to help decipher the many intricate laws that affect notarization. In so doing, the *Primer* will acquaint you with all of the important aspects of Illinois Notary law and with prudent notarial practices in general.

The *Illinois Notary Primer* takes you through the myriad of Notary laws and puts them in easy-to-understand terms. Every section of the law is analyzed and explained, as well as topics not covered by Illinois law but nonetheless of vital concern to you as a Notary.

Whether you are about to be commissioned for the first time, or are a longtime Notary, we are sure the *Illinois Notary Primer* will provide you with new insight and understanding.

Milton G. Valera
Chairman
National Notary Association

The Notary Appointment

Additional information about Illinois requirements for Notaries Public is available on the Secretary of State's website. For step-by-step instructions on the commission application process, applicants may also visit NationalNotary.org.

THE NOTARY COMMISSION

Application

Qualifications. To become a Notary Public in the state of Illinois, the applicant must (5 ILCS 312/2-102):

1. Be a citizen of the United States or non-citizen lawfully admitted for permanent residence.

2. Be proficient in the English language.

3. Be a resident of Illinois or work in the state of Illinois and live in a bordering state.

4. Have not been convicted of a felony.

5. Have not had a prior application or commission revoked due to a finding or decision by the Secretary of State.

6.   Be at least 18 years of age and provide date of birth on the application.

7.   Complete a state approved Notary course and pass an exam.

Application Fee. The application fee for an Illinois Notary commission, for both first-time applicants and renewals, is $15 (5 ILCS 312/2-103).

Checks should be made payable to "Secretary of State." Visa, Mastercard and Discover also are accepted (website, "Notary Public Application Checklist").

Application Submission. The application — along with the $15 fee, the Notary bond and the notarized oath of office — is to be submitted to the Illinois Secretary of State's Index Department (5 ILCS 312/2-103, 104, 105).

Non-Residents. A resident of a bordering state who works in Illinois may apply for a commission as an Illinois Notary Public. Such a commission may be issued only if the adjoining state allows residents of Illinois to be commissioned as Notaries Public in that state. Bordering states with such provisions include Kentucky, Iowa, Missouri and Wisconsin (website, "Non-resident Notary Public Application Checklist") (5 ILCS 312/2-101).

Notary Bond

Requirement. An applicant for a notarial commission or electronic notarial commission must purchase a bond in the following amounts:

1.   Applicants seeking to perform only traditional, in-person notarizations — $5,000.

2.   Applicants seeking to perform either remotely or electronically and by means of audio-video communication — $25,000 in addition to the $5,000, or a combined bond of $30,000 (5 ILCS 312/2-105).

Filing the Bond. The bond must be submitted with the Notary Public application (5 ILCS 312/2-105).

Protects Public. The Notary bond protects the public, not the Notary, from a Notary's misconduct or negligence. The bond provides coverage for damages to anyone who suffers financially from a Notary's actions — intentional or not. The surety company will seek compensation from the Notary for any damages it has to pay out on the Notary's behalf.

Liable for All Damages. The Notary and surety company are liable for damages resulting from notarial misconduct (5 ILCS 312/7-101). The surety company is liable only up to the amount of the bond, but the Notary may be found liable for any amount of money.

Errors and Omissions Insurance. Notaries may choose to purchase insurance to cover any unintentional errors or omissions they may make. Notary errors and omissions insurance provides protection for Notaries who are involved in claims or sued for damages resulting from unintentional notarial errors and omissions. In the event of a claim or civil lawsuit, the insurance company will provide and pay for the Notary's legal counsel and absorb any damages levied by a court or agreed to in a settlement, up to the policy coverage limit. Generally, errors and omissions insurance does not cover the Notary for dishonest, fraudulent or criminal acts or omissions, or for willful or intentional disregard of the law.

Reasonable Care

Responsibility. As public servants, Notaries must act responsibly and exercise reasonable care in the performance of their official duties. If a Notary fails to do so, he or she may be subject to a civil suit to recover financial damages caused by the Notary's error.

In general, reasonable care is the degree of attentiveness that a person of normal intelligence and responsibility would exhibit. If a Notary can show a judge or jury that he or she did everything expected of a reasonable person, the judge or jury is obligated by law to find the Notary not liable for damages.

Complying with all pertinent laws is the first rule of reasonable care for a Notary. If there are no statutory guidelines in a given instance, the Notary should exercise common sense and prudence.

Oath of Office

Requirement. Each person applying for a Notary commission must take and sign an oath of office in the presence of a person qualified to administer an oath in Illinois, such as another Notary Public (5 ILCS 312/2-104).

Filing the Oath. The Notary oath of office must be submitted to the Secretary of State along with the Notary bond and application (5 ILCS 312/2-105).

Commission Appointment and Reappointment

Appointment. Once it is determined that an applicant meets all requirements, the Secretary of State will appoint the applicant to the office of Notary Public and issue a Notary commission certificate.

Reappointment. A current Notary may apply for reappointment 60 days before the expiration of an existing commission. The date of the new commission will be the date immediately after the expiration date of the current commission.

To avoid any gaps between Notary commissions, Notary applications should be filed at least 30 days before the expiration of the current commission.

Commission Cancellation. An applicant can request the cancellation of a Notary appointment. The cancellation becomes effective upon receipt by the Secretary of State of the notice requesting the cancellation.

Jurisdiction

Statewide. A person commissioned as an Illinois Notary Public may perform official acts throughout the state of Illinois, as long as the Notary continues to reside or work in the same county in which commissioned (5 ILCS 312/3-105). A Notary may not witness a signing outside Illinois and then return to the state to perform the notarization; all parts of a notarial act must be performed at the same time and place within the state of Illinois.

Term of Office

Four-Year Term. An Illinois Notary Public's term of office is four years (5 ILCS 312/2-101).

Out-of-State Residents. Residents of bordering states whose place of work or business is in the state of Illinois may be commissioned for a term of one year, but only if the laws of the applicant's state of residence authorize residents of Illinois to be appointed and commissioned as Notaries in that state (5 ILCS 312/2-101).

Change of Name, Address, or Email Address

Failure to Notify the Secretary of State. If a Notary legally changes his or her name, changes his or her residential address or business address, or email address, without notifying the Secretary of State in writing within 30 days, the Notary's commission ceases to be in effect.

Resident of Bordering State. If a Notary who is a resident of a state bordering Illinois no longer maintains a principal place of work or principal place of business in the same county in Illinois in which the Notary was commissioned, the commission of that Notary ceases to be in effect.

Commission Termination. Once the commission is terminated an individual who desires to again become a Notary must file a new application, bond, and oath with the Secretary of State (5 ILCS 312/4-101[a]).

Address Change to a New County. If a Notary moves out of the county from which the Notary was appointed, the Notary must resign his or her commission. The Notary can then apply for a new appointment (NPH).

Address Change Within the County. If a Notary moves or changes employers and the new residence or place of employment is within the boundaries of the county in which the Notary was appointed, the Notary must report the change of address to the Secretary of State (NPH).

New Seal. When the commission of a Notary ceases to be in effect, the notarial seal or electronic notary seal must be surrendered to the Secretary of State, and his or her certificate of notarial commission or certificate of electronic notarial commission must be destroyed. ■

Screening the Signer

SCREENING BASICS

Personal Appearance

Requirement. The principal signer must personally appear before the Notary at the time of the notarization. This means that the Notary and the signer must both be physically present, face to face in the same room, when the notarization takes place (INPH).

Notarizations may never be performed over the telephone, and the Notary's familiarity with a signer's signature is never a replacement for that signer's personal appearance.

Willingness

Confirmation. The Notary should make every effort to confirm that the signer is acting willingly.

To confirm willingness, Notaries need only ask document signers if they are signing of their own free will. If a signer does or says anything that makes the Notary think the signer is being pressured to sign, the Notary should refuse to notarize.

Awareness

Confirmation. The Notary should make every effort to confirm that the signer is generally aware of what is taking place.

To confirm awareness, the Notary simply makes a layperson's judgment about the signer's ability to understand what is happening. A document signer who cannot respond intelligibly in a simple conversation with the Notary should not be considered sufficiently aware to sign at that moment. If the notarization is taking place in a medical environment, the signer's doctor can be consulted for a professional opinion. Otherwise, if the signer's awareness is in doubt, the Notary should refuse to notarize.

Identifying Document Signers

Satisfactory Evidence. Under Illinois law, every individual whose signature is notarized must be positively identified by the Notary Public. Each of the following three methods of identification is considered "satisfactory evidence" of an individual's identity (5 ILCS 312/6-102):

1. The Notary's personal knowledge of the signer's identity. (See "Personal Knowledge of Identity," below.)

2. Reliable identification documents or ID cards as defined by statute. (See "Identification Documents," pages 10–11.)

3. The oath or affirmation of a personally known credible identifying witness. (See "Credible Identifying Witnesses," pages 11–12.)

Personal Knowledge of Identity

Definition. The safest and most reliable method of identifying a document signer is for the Notary to depend upon his or her own personal knowledge of the signer's identity. Personal knowledge means familiarity with an individual resulting from interactions with that person over a period of time sufficient to eliminate every reasonable doubt that the person has the identity claimed.

Illinois law does not specify how long a Notary must be acquainted with an individual before personal knowledge of identity may be claimed. The Notary's common sense must prevail. In general, the longer the Notary is acquainted with a person, and the more interactions the Notary has had with that person, the more likely the individual is personally known.

Whenever the Notary has a reasonable doubt about a signer's identity, that individual should be considered not personally known, and the identification should be made through either a credible identifying witness or reliable identification documents.

Identification Documents

Acceptable Identification Documents. An identification document used to identify a signer for a notarial act must be valid at the time of notarization, must be issued by a state agency, federal government agency, or consulate, and must contain the photograph and signature of the bearer (5 ILCS 312/6-102[d][3]).

Acceptable identification documents include the following, provided they meet the criteria outlined above:

- Illinois driver's license or non-driver's ID card

- Driver's license or non-driver's ID card from another U.S. state, territory or jurisdiction

- U.S. passport or passport card

- A valid foreign passport

- U.S. military ID card

- ID card issued by the USCIS

Unacceptable Identification Documents. Examples of unacceptable identification documents include Social Security cards, birth certificates and credit cards. Social Security cards and birth certificates, while issued by the government, do not contain a photograph of the bearer. Credit cards, while they may contain the signature and photograph of the individual, are not issued by the government.

Name Variations. The Notary should make sure that the name on the document is the same as the name appearing on the identification presented.

In certain circumstances, it may be acceptable for the name on the document to be an abbreviated form of the name on the ID — for example, John D. Smith instead of John David Smith. Last names or surnames, however, should always be the same.

Multiple Identification. While one good identification document or card is sufficient to identify a signer, the Notary may ask for more.

Fraudulent Identification. Identification documents are the least secure of the three methods of identifying a document signer, because phony ID cards are common. The Notary should scrutinize each card for evidence of tampering or counterfeiting, or for evidence that it is a genuine card that has been issued to an impostor.

Some clues that an ID card may have been fraudulently altered include mismatched type styles, a photograph with a raised surface, a signature that does not match the signature on the document, unauthorized lamination of the card, and smudges, erasures, smears and discolorations.

Possible tip-offs to a counterfeit ID card include misspelled words, a brand new-looking card with an old date of issuance, two cards with exactly the same photograph showing the bearer in identical clothing or with an identical background, and inappropriate patterns and features.

Indications that an identification card may have been issued to an impostor include the birthdate or address on the card being unfamiliar to the bearer and all the ID cards seeming brand new.

Credible Identifying Witnesses

Purpose. When the person signing the document is not personally known to the Notary and is not able to present reliable ID cards, that signer may be identified on the oath or affirmation of a credible identifying witness.

Credible Witness Qualifications. Illinois law requires that a credible identifying witness be personally known to the Notary (5 ILCS 312/6-102[d]). In addition, the witness must personally know the person signing the document well enough to swear or affirm that the signer is who he or she claims to be. This creates a chain of personal knowledge from the Notary to the credible identifying witness to the signer. In a sense, a credible identifying witness is a walking, talking ID card.

A reliable credible identifying witness should have a reputation for honesty. The witness should be a competent individual who will not be tricked, cajoled, bullied or otherwise influenced into identifying someone he or she does not really know. In addition, the witness should have no personal interest in the transaction.

Wording for Oath (Affirmation). An oath or affirmation must be administered to the credible identifying witness by the Notary to compel truthfulness. If not otherwise prescribed by Illinois law, an acceptable credible-witness oath or affirmation might be:

> Do you solemnly swear that you know this signer truly is the person he/she claims to be, so help you God?

> (Do you solemnly affirm that you know this signer truly is the person he/she claims to be?)

Blind Signers

Notary Must Read the Document. In the State of Illinois, a Notary may not take the acknowledgment of any person who is blind until the Notary has read the document to the person (5 ILCS 312/6-104[e]).

Adjudged Mentally Ill Signers

Must Refuse Notarization. A Notary may not take the acknowledgment of or administer an oath to any person whom the Notary actually knows to have been adjudged mentally ill by a court of competent jurisdiction and who has not been restored to mental health as a matter of record (5 ILCS 312/6-104[d]).

Persons Physically Unable to Sign

Person Unable to Sign. When a person cannot physically sign a document they may direct a another person, other than the Notary, to sign the person's name on the document. Both the principal and the person directed to sign the document must appear before the Notary at the time the document is signed (Section 176.610).

Notary Statement. A Notary who performs a notarial act for a person who cannot physically sign, must type, print or stamp the following, or a substantially similar statement near the signature "Signature affixed by (name of individual) at the direction of (name of person physically unable to sign)".

Certificate Wording. The following certificate wording is sufficient for an acknowledgment by a person who is physically unable to sign a document:

State of Illinois

County of _____

This instrument was acknowledged before me on_____, day of _____, 20_____ by (printed name of person who cannot physically sign the document) who directed that the affiant's signature be affixed to the above instrument by...(name of person directed to sign the document).

(Signature of notarial officer)_____

(Seal)

Notarizing for Minors

Under Age 18. Generally, persons must reach the age of majority before they can handle their own legal affairs and sign documents for themselves. In Illinois, the age of majority is 18. Normally, natural guardians (parents) or court-appointed guardians will sign on a minor's behalf. In certain cases, where minors are engaged in a business transaction or serving as court witnesses, they may lawfully sign documents and have their signatures notarized. In these cases, the minor must provide proof of identity, and a parent or legal guardian should be present (INHP).

Include Age Next to Signature. When notarizing for a minor, the Notary should ask the minor signer to write his or her age next to the signature to alert any person relying on the document that the signer is a minor. The Notary is not required to verify the minor signer's age.

Identification. The method for identifying a minor is the same as that for an adult. However, determining the identity of a minor can be a problem because minors often do not possess acceptable identification documents, such as driver licenses or passports. If the minor does not have acceptable ID, then one of the other methods of identifying signers must be used, either the Notary's personal knowledge of the minor or the oath of a credible identifying witness who can identify the minor. (See "Identifying Document Signers," page 9.) ■

Reviewing the Document

DOCUMENT ELIGIBILITY

Blank or Incomplete Documents

Do Not Notarize. Illinois Notaries may not notarize blank or incomplete documents (INPH). Any blanks in a document should be filled in by the signer prior to notarization. If the blanks are inapplicable and intended to be left unfilled, the signer should line through each space or write "Not Applicable" or "N/A." The Notary may not, however, tell the signer what to write in the blanks. If the signer is unsure how to fill in the blanks, he or she should contact the document's issuer, its eventual recipient, or an attorney.

Photocopies & Faxes

Original Signature. A photocopy or fax may be notarized as long as the signature on it is original, meaning that the photocopy or fax must have been signed with pen and ink. Signatures on documents presented for notarization must always be signed with a handwritten, original signature. A photocopied or faxed signature may never be notarized.

Public recorders sometimes will not accept notarized photocopies or faxes, because the text of the document may be too faint to adequately reproduce in microfilming.

Foreign Languages

Foreign-Language Advertisements. Notaries who are not attorneys or accredited immigration representatives who advertise notarial services in any language(s) other than English must prominently post in their place of business a schedule of notarial fees in both English and the other language(s). They also must post with the advertisement the following statement, in English and in the same language(s) as the advertisement:

> "I AM NOT AN ATTORNEY LICENSED TO PRACTICE LAW IN ILLINOIS. I AM NOT ALLOWED TO DRAFT LEGAL DOCUMENTS OR RECORDS, NOR MAY I GIVE LEGAL ADVICE ON ANY MATTER, INCLUDING, BUT NOT LIMITED TO, MATTERS OF IMMIGRATION, OR ACCEPT OR CHARGE FEES FOR THE PERFORMANCE OF THOSE ACTIVITIES."

If the advertisement is by radio or television, the statement may be modified but must include substantially the same message.

A Notary who is subject to the foreign-language advertising requirement must provide to persons seeking notarial services an acknowledgment form reciting the legal notice in substantially the same form as the statement required for written and electronic advertisements, and must have the person seeking notarial services sign the form; and further provides that the Notary must provide a copy of the signed form to the person and retain a copy of the signed form throughout their current commission and for 2 years thereafter. The acknowledgment form will be translated by the Secretary of State into Spanish and any other language the Secretary deems necessary and provided on the Secretary's website. Violations of the foreign-language advertisement provisions are punishable by a $1,500 fine for each offense and permanent revocation of the Notary's commission upon the second violation. In addition, the Notary may be subject to other civil or criminal-penalties (5 ILCS 312/3-103).

Finally, a Notary may not in any advertisement use the literal translation from English to any other language terms or titles including, but not limited to, "Notary Public," "Notary," "licensed," "attorney," "lawyer" or any other term that implies that the person is an attorney (5 ILCS 312/3-103).

Foreign-Language Documents. Although Illinois Notaries are not expressly prohibited from notarizing documents written in a language they cannot read, there are difficulties and dangers in doing so: The document may be misrepresented to the Notary, a blatant fraud may go undetected, the Notary may inadvertently perform an incorrect or illegal notarial act, and making a complete journal entry may be difficult. Ideally, a foreign-language document should be referred to a Notary who reads that language.

If a Notary chooses to notarize a document that he or she cannot read, then the Notary certificate should be in English or in a language the Notary can read, and the signature being notarized should be written in characters the Notary is familiar with.

Foreign-Language Signers. Illinois statute specifies that, if a signer does not speak or understand English, the "nature and effect" of the document must be translated into a language that the person does understand before the document can be notarized (5 ILCS 312/6-104[f]).

The best course of action is to refer the signer to a bilingual Notary, since there should always be direct communication between the Notary and document signer — whether in English or any other language. The Notary should never rely upon an intermediary or interpreter to be assured that a signer is willing and aware, given that the third party may have a motive for misrepresenting the circumstances to the Notary and/or the signer.

Immigration

Permitted Services. A Notary Public who is not an attorney or an immigration representative accredited by the Board of Immigration Appeals may provide limited immigration assistance services. Such services specifically exclude giving legal advice, recommending a specific course of legal action, or providing any other assistance that requires legal analysis, legal judgment, or interpretation of the law (815 ILCS 505/2AA[a]).

Prohibited Actions. Non-attorney Notaries may not represent themselves to be experts on immigration matters or provide any other assistance that requires legal analysis, legal judgment, or interpretation of the law unless they are a designated entity as defined by the Code of Federal Regulations or an entity accredited by the Board of Immigration Appeals (5 ILCS 312/3-103[c]).

Wills

Do Not Offer Advice. Often, people attempt to draw up wills on their own without benefit of legal counsel and then bring these homemade testaments to a Notary to have them "legalized," expecting the Notary to know how to proceed. In advising or assisting such persons, the Notary risks prosecution for the unauthorized practice of law. The Notary's ill-informed advice also may do considerable damage to the affairs of the signer and subject the Notary to a civil lawsuit.

Wills are highly sensitive documents, the format of which is strictly dictated by laws. The slightest deviation from these laws can nullify a will. In some cases, holographic (handwritten) wills have actually been voided by notarization because the document was not entirely in the handwriting of the testator.

Do Not Notarize Without Certificate Wording. A Notary should notarize a document described as a will only if a Notary certificate is provided or stipulated for each signer, and the signers are not asking questions about how to proceed. Any such questions should properly be answered by an attorney.

Living Wills. Documents that are popularly called "living wills" may be notarized. These are not actually wills at all, but written statements of the signer's wishes concerning medical treatment in the event that person has an illness or injury and is unable to issue instructions on his or her own behalf.

Certificate of Authority

Documents Sent Out of State. Documents notarized in Illinois and sent out of state may be required to bear proof that the Notary's signature and seal are genuine and that the Notary had authority to act at the time of notarization. In Illinois, the process of proving the genuineness of an official signature and seal is called a Certificate of Authority.

A Certificate of Authority for an Illinois Notary may be obtained at the office of the county clerk where the Notary's commission has been recorded. Certificates of Authority for Notaries are also issued by the Illinois Secretary of State's office (5 ILCS 312/3-106).

Certificates of Authority are known by many different names: certificates of official character, authenticating certificates, certificates of capacity, certificates of prothonotary and "flags."

Anyone who requires Certificates of Authority should contact the county clerk or the Secretary of State's Index Department. It is not the responsibility of the Notary Public to obtain certification.

The fee for a certificate of authority is $2. Certifications may be obtained by mail or in person from:

> Office of Secretary of State
> Index Department
> Notary Public
> Division 111 East
> Monroe Street
> Springfield, IL 62756
> (217) 782-7017

For notarized documents sent from Illinois to other U.S. states and jurisdictions, a single authenticating certificate from the county clerk or Illinois Secretary of State is normally sufficient authentication.

Documents Sent Out of the Country. If the notarized document is going outside the United States, a chain authentication process may be necessary, and additional authenticating certificates may have to be obtained from the U.S. Department of State in Washington, D.C., a foreign consulate, and a ministry of foreign affairs in the particular foreign nation.

***Apostilles* and The Hague Convention.** More than 100 nations, including the United States, subscribe to a treaty under the auspices of The Hague Conference that simplifies authentication of notarized documents exchanged between these nations. The official name of this treaty, adopted by the Conference on October 5, 1961, is *The Hague Convention Abolishing the Requirement of Legalization for Foreign Public Documents.* (For a list of the subscribing countries, visit www.hcch.net/index_en.php.)

Under The Hague Convention, only one authenticating certificate called an apostille is necessary to ensure acceptance in these subscribing countries. (*Apostille* is French for "notation.")

In Illinois, *apostilles* are issued by the Secretary of State (15 ILCS 305/5.20).

Disqualifying Interest

Impartiality. Notaries are commissioned by the state to be impartial, disinterested witnesses whose screening duties help ensure the integrity of important legal and commercial transactions. Lack of impartiality by a Notary throws doubt on the integrity and lawfulness of any transaction.

Illinois statutes specify that a Notary may not notarize any instrument in which the Notary's name appears as a party to the transaction (5 ILCS 312/6-104[b]). In addition, a Notary must never notarize his or her own signature (INPH).

Financial or Beneficial Interest. A Notary should not perform any notarization related to a transaction in which that Notary has a direct financial or beneficial interest. A financial or beneficial interest exists when the Notary is named as a principal in a financial transaction or when the Notary receives an advantage, right, privilege, property or fee valued in excess of the lawfully prescribed notarial fee.

In regard to real estate transactions, a Notary is generally considered to have a disqualifying financial or beneficial interest when that Notary is a grantor or grantee, mortgagor or mortgagee, trustor or trustee, lessor or lessee or a beneficiary of the transaction.

Relatives. Although Illinois state law does not expressly prohibit notarizing for a relative, the National Notary Association strongly advises against doing so for persons related by blood or marriage. Family matters often involve a financial or other beneficial interest that may not be readily apparent at the time of notarization.

Notarizing for family members also may test the Notary's ability to act impartially. For example, a Notary who is asked to notarize a contract signed by his or her brother might attempt to persuade him to sign or not sign. A sibling is entitled to exert influence, but this is entirely improper for a Notary.

Even if a Notary has no interest in the document and does not attempt to influence the signer, notarizing for a relative could subject the document to a legal challenge if other parties to the transaction allege the Notary could not have acted impartially.

Unauthorized Practice of Law

Prohibited. Non-attorney Notaries may never prepare any legal document or fill in the blanks of a document for another person, although they of course may complete the Notary certificate on any document (5 ILCS 312/6-104[h]). As private individuals, they also are free to prepare and complete legal documents to which they are personally a party. They may not, however, notarize their own signature on such documents.

Explaining Documents. A Notary may not explain, certify or verify the contents of a document. However a Notary who is also an attorney is not prohibited from notarizing a document prepared by that attorney (5 ILCS 312/6-104[k]).

Notaries who are not attorneys or accredited immigration representatives may not accept payment in exchange for providing legal advice or any other assistance that requires legal analysis, legal judgment, or interpretation of the law (5 ILCS 312/3-103[e]).

Exceptions. Non-attorney Notaries who are specially trained, certified or licensed in a particular field (e.g., real estate, insurance and escrow) may advise others about documents in that field, but in no other. In addition, trained paralegals under the supervision of an attorney may advise others about documents in legal matters.

Refusal of Service

Notary May Refuse. According to Illinois law, Notaries have no obligation to perform any notarial or electronic notarial act, and may refuse to perform a notarization without further explanation (5 ILCS 312/6-102/ 6-102[e]).

Business Hours. Notaries are not expected to be available to notarize for the public other than during the Notary's normal business hours. However, a Notary may elect to offer notarial services at any hour. ■

Notary Acts

Authorized Acts

Notaries may perform the following Notary acts (5 ILCS 255/2, 5 ILCS 312/6-101, 765 ILCS 30/2 and INPH):

- **Acknowledgments,** certifying that a signer personally appeared before the Notary, was positively identified by the Notary and acknowledged freely signing the document. (See pages 24–26.)

- **Oaths and Affirmations,** solemn promises to a Supreme Being (oaths) or on one's own personal honor (affirmations) spoken in the Notary's presence. (See pages 26 –27.)

- **Verifications Upon Oath or Affirmation,** as found in affidavits and other sworn documents, certifying that the signer personally appeared before the Notary, was positively identified by the Notary, signed in the Notary's presence and took an oath or affirmation from the Notary. (See pages 27–29.)

- **Witnessing or Attesting Signatures,** certifying that a signer personally appeared before the Notary, was positively identified by the Notary and signed the document in the Notary's presence. (See page 32–33.)

- **Certifying or Attesting Copies** certifies that a photocopy of an original document is a true and complete copy (see pages 29–30).

- **Certifying a Paper Printout of an Electronic Document** certifies that a paper or tangible copy of an electronic document is a true and correct copy of an electronic document (see pages 30–31).

- **Proofs of Execution by Subscribing Witness,** certifying that a subscribing witness personally appeared and swore to the Notary that another person, the principal, signed a document. (See pages 33–35.)

- **Protests,** noting protests of negotiable instruments.

Acknowledgments

Purpose. Acknowledgments are one of the most common forms of notarization. In Illinois, whenever any deed or instrument conveying real estate is to be made a matter of record, the signatures of the parties making the conveyance must be acknowledged before a Notary or other authorized officer (765 ILCS 5/35c). The primary purpose of an acknowledgment is to positively identify the document signer.

Procedure. In executing an acknowledgment, the Notary certifies three things (5 ILCS 312/6-101[b], 5 ILCS 312/6-102[a] and 765 ILCS 30/4):

1. The signer *personally appeared* before the Notary on the date and in the county indicated on the Notary certificate.

2. The signer was *positively identified* by the Notary through personal knowledge or other satisfactory evidence. (See "Identifying Document Signers," page 9.)

3. The signer *acknowledged* to the Notary that the signature was freely made for the purposes stated in the document and, if the document is signed in a representative capacity, that he or she had the proper authority to do so. (If a document is willingly signed in the presence of the Notary, this act has the same effect as an oral statement of acknowledgment.)

Identification of Signer. In executing an acknowledgment, the Notary must identify the signer through personal knowledge or another form of satisfactory evidence (5 ILCS 312/6-102a). (See "Identifying Document Signers," page 9.)

Witnessing Signature Not Required. For an acknowledgment, the document need not be signed in the Notary's presence. The document may be signed prior to the notarization (an hour before, a week before, a year before, etc.) as long as the signer appears with the document before the Notary at the time of notarization and acknowledges having signed (INPH).

Representative Capacity. A person may sign and Acknowledge a document in any lawful representative capacity on behalf of another person or a legal entity. Specifically, a person may sign in one of the following capacities (5 ILCS 312/6-101):

- For and on behalf of a corporation, partnership, trust or other entity, as an authorized officer, agent, partner, trustee or other representative.

- As a public officer, personal representative, guardian or other representative in the specific capacity described in the document.

- As an attorney in fact for a principal signer or in any other capacity as an authorized representative of another.

Certificates for Acknowledgment. Illinois law provides acknowledgment certificates for individuals signing on their own behalf, plus a short-form acknowledgment certificate for signers in various representative capacities (5 ILCS 312/6-105).

- For an acknowledgment in an individual capacity:

State of Illinois

County of _____

This instrument was acknowledged before me on _____ (date) by _____ (name[s] of person[s]).

(Seal) _____ (Signature of Notary Public)

- For an acknowledgment in a representative capacity:

State of Illinois

County of _____

This instrument was acknowledged before me on _____
(date) by _____ (name[s] of person[s]) as (type
of authority, e.g., officer, trustee, etc.) of _____
(name of party on behalf of whom instrument was executed).

(Seal) _____ (Signature of Notary Public)

Oaths and Affirmations

Purpose. An oath is a solemn, spoken pledge to a Supreme Being. An affirmation is a solemn, spoken pledge on one's own personal honor, with no reference to a Supreme Being. Both are usually a promise of truthfulness and have the same legal effect.

In taking an oath or affirmation in an official proceeding, a person may be subject to criminal penalties for perjury should he or she fail to be truthful.

An oath or affirmation can be a full-fledged notarial act in its own right, as when giving an oath of office to a public official, or it can be part of the process of notarizing a document (e.g., taking a verification upon oath or affirmation or swearing in a credible identifying witness).

A person who objects to taking an oath may instead be given an affirmation.

Wording for Oaths (Affirmations). If the law does not dictate otherwise, an Illinois Notary may use the following or similar words in administering an oath (or affirmation):

- Oath (affirmation) for an affiant signing an affidavit or a deponent signing a deposition:

Do you solemnly swear that the statements made in this document are true to the best of your knowledge and belief, so help you God?

(Do you solemnly affirm that the statements in this document are true to the best of your knowledge and belief?)

- Oath (affirmation) for a credible identifying witness:

  Do you solemnly swear that you know this signer truly is the person he/she claims to be, so help you God?

  (Do you solemnly affirm that you know this signer truly is the person he/she claims to be?)

- Oath (affirmation) for a subscribing witness:

  Do you solemnly swear that you saw (name of the document signer) sign his/her name to this document and/or that he/she acknowledged to you having executed it for the purposes therein stated, so help you God?

  (Do you solemnly affirm that you saw [name of the document signer] sign his/her name to this document and/or that he/she acknowledged to you having executed it for the purposes therein stated?)

The oath or affirmation wording must be spoken aloud, and the oath-taker or affirmant must answer with "I do," "Yes" or the like. A nod or grunt is not a sufficient response. If a person is unable to speak, the Notary may rely upon written notes to communicate.

Ceremony and Gestures. To impress upon the person taking the oath or affirmation the importance of truthfulness, the Notary is encouraged to lend a sense of ceremony and formality to the oath or affirmation. During administration of an oath or affirmation, the Notary and the person taking the oath or affirmation may raise their right hands, though this is not a legal requirement. Notaries generally have discretion to use the words and gestures that they feel will most compellingly appeal to the conscience of the person taking the oath or affirmation.

Verification Upon Oath or Affirmation

Purpose. In notarizing affidavits and other documents signed and sworn to before an oath-administering official, the Notary normally executes a verification upon oath or affirmation.

The main purpose of a verification upon oath or affirmation is to compel truthfulness by appealing to the signer's conscience and fear of criminal penalties for perjury.

Procedure. In executing a verification upon oath or affirmation, a Notary certifies four things (5 ILCS 312/6-101[c], 5 ILCS 312/6-102[b] and INPH):

1. The signer *personally appeared* before the Notary on the date and in the county indicated on the Notary certificate.

2. The signer was *positively identified* by the Notary through personal knowledge or other satisfactory evidence. (See "Identifying Document Signers," pages 18–21.)

3. The Notary *watched the signer sign* the document at the time of notarization.

4. The Notary administered an *oath or affirmation* to the signer.

Identification of Signer. In executing a verification upon oath or affirmation, the Notary must identify the signer through personal knowledge or another form of satisfactory evidence (5 ILCS 312/ 6-102b). (See "Identifying Document Signers," page 9.)

Wording for Oath (Affirmation). If not otherwise prescribed by law, an Illinois Notary may use the following or similar words to administer an oath (or affirmation) in conjunction with a verification upon or affirmation:

> Do you solemnly swear that the statements in this document are true to the best of your knowledge and belief, so help you God?

> (Do you solemnly affirm that the statements in this document are true to the best of your knowledge and belief?)

The signer must respond aloud and affirmatively with "I do," "Yes" or the like.

Certificate for Verification Upon Oath or Affirmation. This notarial act requires a certificate called a jurat. The following jurat wording is sufficient for all verifications upon oath or affirmation (5 ILCS 312/6-105[c]):

State of Illinois

County of _____

Signed and sworn (or affirmed) to before me on _____ (date) by _____ (name[s] of person[s] making statement).

(Seal)   _____ (Signature of Notary Public)

Representative Capacity. Verifications upon oath or affirmation may be made in a representative capacity (INPH). An individual may personally vouch for the truthfulness of a statement as a representative of a corporation, partnership, trust or other entity, as an attorney in fact or as a public officer, representative or guardian. Strictly speaking, oaths and affirmations taken in a representative capacity are the acts of the person making them. They must be made based upon the knowledge of the person taking the oath or affirmation.

State of Illinois

County of _____

Signed and sworn (or affirmed) to before me on _____ (date) by _____ (name of person) as (type of authority, e.g., officer, trustee, etc.) of _____ (name of party on behalf of whom instrument was executed).

(Seal)   _____ (Signature of Notary Public)

Copy Certification

Purpose. Illinois Notaries have the authority to certify that a copy of a document is a true and correct copy of the document presented (5 ILCS 312/1-104).

Procedure. Typically, the permanent custodian of the original document presents the document to the Notary and requests a copy certification, then the Notary takes the document and makes the photocopy. Alternatively, the Notary could supervise the making of the photocopy if the Notary determines that the copy is an accurate and complete copy of the document presented.

Precautions. A Notary may not certify copies of vital records, U.S. Naturalization Certificates or any other record which is prohibited by law to copy or certify.

Certificate. The following is an example of certificate wording for copy certification:

State of Illinois

County of _____

I certify that this is a true and correct copy of a record in the possession of _____ (name of individual).

Date: _____

(Seal)   _____ (Signature of Notary Public)

Certifying a Paper Printout of an Electronic Document

Illinois Notaries have the authority to certify that a paper or tangible copy of an electronic document is a true and correct copy if the Notary has:

1. reasonably confirmed that the electronic document is in a tamper evident format;

2. detected no changes or errors in any electronic signature or other information in the electronic document;

3. personally printed or supervised the printing of the electronic document onto paper or other tangible medium; and

4. not made any changes or modifications to the electronic document or to the paper or tangible copy thereof other than the certification described in this section (765 ILCS 33/3.5(b)).

Certificate. A notarial certificate in substantially the following form is sufficient for certifying a tangible copy of an electronic document:

State of _____

County of _____

On this _____ (date), I certify that the foregoing and annexed
document entitled _____(title) and containing_____
(number of pages) pages is a true and correct copy of an electronic
document printed by me or under my supervision. I further certify
that, at the time of printing, no security features present on the
electronic document indicated any changes or errors in an electronic
signature or other information in the electronic document since its
creation or execution.

(Seal)   _____ (Signature of Notary Public)

Does Not Apply to Plat Maps and Records. This certification does
not apply to any map or plat governed by the Plat Act, the Judicial
Plat Act, or the Permanent Survey Act, or to any monument record
governed by the Land Survey Monuments Act.

Depositions and Affidavits

Purpose. A deposition is a signed transcript of the signer's oral
statements taken down for use in a judicial proceeding. The deposition signer is called the deponent .

An affidavit is a signed written statement made under oath or
affirmation and is used for a variety of purposes both in and out
of court. The signer of an affidavit is called the affiant.

Depositions. With a deposition, both sides in a lawsuit or court
case have the opportunity to cross-examine the deponent. Questions and answers are transcribed into a written statement, and
then signed and sworn to before an oath-administering official
(5 ILCS 255/2).

Illinois Notaries have the power to take depositions, but this duty
is most often executed by trained and certified court reporters.

Affidavits. Affidavits are used in and out of court for a variety
of purposes, from submitting losses to an insurance company to

declaring U.S. citizenship before traveling to a foreign country. If used in a judicial proceeding, an affidavit is submitted in lieu of direct testimony. Instead of appearing in court to be deposed, the affiant submits his or her sworn written statement.

Wording for Oath (Affirmation). If no other wording is prescribed in a given instance, a Notary may use the following language in administering an oath (or affirmation) to an affiant or a deponent:

> Do you solemnly swear that the statements made in this document are true to the best of your knowledge and belief, so help you God?
>
> (Do you solemnly affirm that the statements made in this document are true to the best of your knowledge and belief?)

The affiant or deponent must respond aloud and affirmatively with "I do," "Yes" or the like.

Certificate for Depositions and Affidavits. Depositions and affidavits typically require jurat certificates. (See "Verification Upon Oath or Affirmation," pages 27–29.)

Signature Witnessing or Attestation

Purpose. In a signature witnessing, the Notary determines, either from personal knowledge or satisfactory evidence, that the signature on a document is that of the person appearing before the Notary and named in the document.

Witnessing a signature may be used in circumstances where the date of signing is of crucial importance.

A signature witnessing differs from an acknowledgment in that the party relying upon the document will know that the document was signed on a certain date. A signature witnessing differs from a verification upon oath or affirmation in that the signer is merely signing the document, not vouching that the contents of the document are true.

Procedure. In witnessing or attesting a signature, a Notary certifies three things (5 ILCS 312/6-102[c] and INPH):

1. The signer *personally appeared* before the Notary on the date and in the county indicated on the Notary certificate.

2. The signer was *positively identified* by the Notary through personal knowledge or other satisfactory evidence. (See "Identifying Document Signers," page 9.)

3. The Notary *watched the signer sign* the document at the time of notarization.

Certificate for Signature Witnessing. Illinois statute provides the following wording for witnessing or attesting a signature (5 ILCS 312/6-105[d]):

State of Illinois

County of _____

Signed or attested before me on _____ (date) by
_____ (name[s] of person[s]).

(Seal)   _____ (Signature of Notary Public)

Proof of Execution by Subscribing Witness

Purpose. In executing a proof of execution by subscribing witness, a Notary certifies that the signature of a person who does not appear before the Notary — the principal signer — is genuine and freely made based upon the sworn testimony of another person who does appear — a subscribing (signing) witness.

Proofs of execution are used when the principal signer is out of town or otherwise unavailable to appear before a Notary. Because of their high potential for fraudulent abuse, proofs of execution are not universally accepted.

Prudence dictates that proofs only be used as a last resort and never merely because the principal signer prefers not to take the time to personally appear before a Notary.

In Lieu of Acknowledgment. On recordable documents, a proof of execution by a subscribing witness is usually regarded as an acceptable substitute for an acknowledgment (765 ILCS 30/2 and 765 ILCS 5/20).

Identifying Subscribing Witness. Since the Notary is relying entirely upon the word of the subscribing witness to vouch for an absent signer's identity, willingness and general awareness, it is best for subscribing witnesses to be personally known to the Notary.

Subscribing Witness Qualifications. A subscribing witness is a person who watches the principal sign a document (or who personally takes the principal's acknowledgment) and then subscribes (signs) his or her own name on the document at the principal's request. The witness brings that document to a Notary on the principal's behalf and takes an oath or affirmation from the Notary to the effect that the principal is known to him or her and did willingly sign (or acknowledged signing) the document and request the witness to also sign the document.

The ideal subscribing witness personally knows the principal signer and has no personal beneficial or financial interest in the document or transaction. It would be foolish of the Notary, for example, to rely upon the word of a subscribing witness presenting for notarization a power of attorney that names this very witness as attorney in fact.

Wording for Oath (Affirmation). An acceptable oath (or affirmation) for the subscribing witness might be:

> Do you solemnly swear that you saw (name of the document signer) sign his/her name to this document and/or that he/she acknowledged to you having executed it for the purposes therein stated, so help you God?

> (Do you solemnly affirm that you saw [name of the document signer] sign his/ her name to this document and/or that he/she acknowledged to you having executed it for the purposes therein stated?)

Certificate for Proof of Execution. Illinois statute does not prescribe a Notary certificate for a proof of execution by subscribing witness. When wording is not provided, the National Notary Association recommends the following format for this notarial act:

> State of Illinois   )
>
>   ) ss.
>
> County of _____)

On _____ (date), before me, the undersigned, a Notary Public for the state, personally appeared _____ (subscribing witness's name), personally known to me to be the person whose name is subscribed to the within instrument, as a witness thereto, who, being by me duly sworn, deposes and says that he/she was present and saw _____ (name of principal), the same person described in and whose name is subscribed to the within and annexed instrument in his/her authorized capacity(ies) as a party thereto, execute the same, and that said affiant subscribed his/her name to the within instrument as a witness at the request of _____ (name of principal).

(Seal)   _____ (Signature of Notary Public)

Fees for Notarial Acts

Maximum Fees. The following maximum fees for performing notarial acts are allowed by Illinois law (5 ILCS 312/3-104):

- **Acknowledgments — $5.** For taking an acknowledgment, the Notary may charge no more than $5 for each signature notarized.

- **Oaths and Affirmations Without Signature — $5.** For administering an oath or affirmation without requiring the person taking the oath or affirmation to sign a document, the Notary may charge no more than $5 per oath or affirmation.

- **Verification Upon Oath or Affirmation — $5.** For taking a verification upon oath or affirmation, the Notary may charge no more than $5 for each signature. (This fee includes administration of the oath or affirmation.)

- **Signature Witnessing — $5.** For signature witnessing, the Notary may charge no more than $5.

- **All Other Non-Electronic Notarial Acts — $5.**

- **Electronic Notarial Act — $25.** For performing an electronic notarial act, the Notary may charge $25.

Fees for Immigration Forms. A Notary Public who is not an attorney or an immigration representative accredited by the Board of

Immigration Appeals may provide limited immigration assistance services. Such services specifically exclude giving legal advice, recommending a specific course of legal action, or providing any other assistance that requires legal analysis, legal judgment, or interpretation of the law (815 ILCS 505/2AA[a]). The fees for a Notary, agency, or any other person who is not an attorney or an accredited representative filling out immigration forms is limited to the following (5 ILCS 312/3-104):

- $10 per form for completing immigration forms

- $10 per page for performing required translations on immigration forms

- $5 for performing a notarization

- $3 for obtaining a document required to complete an immigration form

- $75 for completing all tasks related to a single application

Records and Receipts for Fees. Notaries must provide itemized receipts and keep records for fees accepted for services provided. Notarial fees must appear on the itemized receipt as separate and distinct from any other charges assessed (5 ILCS 312/3-104(e)).

Fee Schedule. A Notary who advertises in a language other than English must post a a schedule of the fees in a conspicuous location at all times (5 ILCS 312/3-103).

Option Not to Charge. Notaries are not required to charge for their notarial services, and they may charge any fee less than the statutory maximum.

Travel Fees. Charges for travel by a Notary are not specified by law. Such fees are proper only if the Notary and signer agree beforehand on the amount to be charged. The signer must understand that a travel fee is not stipulated in law and is separate from the notarial fees described above. ■

Recordkeeping

Journal of Notarial Acts

Required. Every Illinois Notary must record each notarial act in a journal at the time of notarization (see page 41 for exceptions). The journal can be either paper or electronic (5 ILCS 312/3-107).

Purpose. Prudent Notaries keep detailed and accurate journals of their notarial acts for many reasons:

- Keeping records is a businesslike practice that every conscientious businessperson and public official should exercise. Not keeping records of important transactions, whether private or public, is risky.

- A Notary's journal protects the public's rights to valuable property and to due process by providing documentary evidence in the event a document is lost or altered, or if a transaction is later challenged.

- In the event of a civil lawsuit alleging that the Notary's negligence or misconduct caused the plaintiff financial harm, a detailed journal of notarial acts can protect the Notary by showing that reasonable care was used to identify a signer. It would be difficult to contend that the Notary did not bother to identify a signer if the Notary's journal contained a detailed description of the ID cards that the signer presented.

- Since civil lawsuits arising from a contested notarial act typically take place three to six years after the act occurs, the Notary normally cannot accurately testify in court about the particulars of a notarization without a journal to aid his or her memory.

- Journals of notarial acts can prevent baseless lawsuits by showing that a Notary did use reasonable care or that a transaction did occur as recorded. Journal thumbprints and signatures are especially effective in defeating such groundless suits.

Requirements. Each journal must contain all of the following information (Section 176.900):

1. The name of the Notary as it appears on the commission;

2. The Notary's commission number;

3. The Notary's commission expiration date;

4. The Notary's office address of record with the Secretary of State;

5. A statement that, upon the death or adjudication of incompetency of the Notary, the Notary's personal representative or guardian or any other person knowingly in possession of the journal must deliver or mail it to the Secretary of State;

6. The meaning of any abbreviated word or symbol used in recording a notarial act in the notarial journal; and

7. The signature of the Notary

Required Journal Entries. Each journal entry must contain the following information (Section 176.900):

1. The name of the principal;

2. The name of each credible witness;

3. The name of any other person that signed for the principal;

4. The title or a description of the document notarized;

5. The date of the notarization;

6. Whether the notarization was conducted in person, remotely, or electronically;

7. The notarial fee charged, if any.

8. The physical location of the Notary and the principal.

Fees. Each fee recorded in the journal should correspond to the notarial act performed. If no fee is charged, the Notary must indicate so in the journal. Clerical and administrative fees, if charged, must be separately itemized.

Address. For journal entries, the address indicates the city and state only.

Optional Entries. In addition to the required entries, a journal may contain the signature of the signer and any additional information about a specific transaction that might assist the Notary to recall the transaction.

Prohibited Entries. A Notary is prohibited from recording the following information in the journal:

1. An identification number assigned by a governmental agency or by the United States that is on the identification card or passport presented as identification;

2. Any other number that could be used to identify the principal of the document;

3. A biometric identifier, including a fingerprint, voice print or retina image of the principal; and

4. An individual's first name or first initial and last name in combination with and linked to any one or more of the following elements when the elements are not encrypted or redacted:

    A. Social Security number;

    B. Driver's license number or a State identification card number; or

C. Financial account information; and

5. An electronic signature of the person for whom an electronic notarial act was performed or any witnesses

Inadvertent or Accidental Entries. If a Notary inadvertently records prohibited information in the journal, the Notary must redact the information before providing pubic access or copies of the journal.

Multiple Notarizations for Same Principal. Multiple notarizations for the same principal within a single transaction may be abbreviated in the journal. The first notarization must include all the required information listed above and abbreviated entries must indicate the type of transaction and the number of documents notarized as part of that single transaction (Section 176.920).

Document Dates. If the document has a specific date on it, the Notary should record that date in the journal of notarial acts. Often the only date on a document is the date of the signature that is being notarized. If the signature is undated, however, the document may have no date on it at all. In that case, the Notary should record "no date" or "undated" in the journal.

For acknowledgments, the date the document was signed must either precede or be the same as the date of the notarization; it may not follow it. For a verification upon oath or affirmation, the date the document was signed and the date of the notarization must be the same.

A document whose signature is dated after the date on its Notary certificate risks rejection by a recorder, who may question how the document could have been notarized before it was signed.

Journal Signature. Although not required by Illinois law, perhaps the most important entry to obtain is the signer's signature. A journal signature protects the Notary against claims that a signer did not appear and is a deterrent to forgery, because it provides evidence of the signer's identity and appearance before the Notary. Electronic signatures for electronic notarizations, however, are prohibited by law (5 ILCS 312/3-107).

To check for possible forgery, the Notary should compare the signature that the person leaves in the journal of notarial acts with the signatures on the document and on the IDs. The signatures should be at least reasonably similar.

The Notary also should observe the signing of the journal. If the signer appears to be laboring over the journal signature, this may be an indication of forgery in progress.

Since a journal signature is not required by law, the Notary may not refuse to notarize if the signer declines to leave one.

Complete Entry Before Certificate. The prudent Notary completes the journal entry before filling out the Notary certificate on a document. This prevents the signer from leaving with the notarized document before vital information can be entered in the journal.

Journal Exception — Notary Employed by Attorney. A Notary employed by an attorney or law firm is not required to keep a journal of notarizations performed during the notary's employment if the attorney or law firm maintains a copy of the documents notarized (IAC 176.900 (f)).

Journal Exception — Election Documents. A Notary is not required to record notarial acts performed for the following election documents to be filed by or on behalf of a candidate for public office (5 ILCS 312/3-107 (f):

1. nominating petitions;

2. petitions of candidacy;

3. petitions for nomination;

4. nominating papers; or

5. nomination papers.

Never Surrender Journal. The journal is the personal property of the Notary, regardless of who paid for it. A Notary must not surrender the journal to an employer upon termination of employment and an employer may not retain the journal of an employee when the employment of the Notary ceases.

Journal Retention. A journal maintained in a tangible format must be retained for a minimum of 7 years after the final notarial act chronicled in the journal. Retention requirements do not apply to Notaries in the course of their employment with a governmental entity.

Journal Inspection. Because a journal is a public record, any person may inspect a journal entry in the Notary's presence during the notary's regular business hours, but only if (Section 176.950(a)):

1. The person's identity is personally known to the notary or proven through satisfactory evidence;

2. The person affixes a signature in the journal in a separate, dated entry;

3. The person specifies the month, year, type of document, and the name of the principal for the notarial act or acts sought; and

4. The person is shown only the entry or entries specified.

Inspection Denial. If a Notary has a reasonable and explainable belief that a person has a criminal or harmful intent in requesting information from the journal, the Notary may deny access to any entry (Section 176.950(b)).

Attorney-Client Privilege. Journals of notarizations performed solely within the course of a Notary's employment with an attorney or law firm are the property of the employing attorney or firm. An attorney or law firm is not required to violate attorney-client privilege by allowing or authorizing inspection of any notarizations that are recorded in a Notary's journal (IAC 176.900 f)).

Subpoenas and Investigative Requests. A request for inspection or certified copies of a journal made through an investigative request by law enforcement or by the Secretary of State or in a subpoena shall be complied with in the manner specified in the request or subpoena (Section 176.95(b)).

Lost, Stolen or Compromised Journal. If a Notary's journal is lost, stolen or compromised, the Notary must notify the Secretary of

State in writing or electronically the next business day after discovery. The Statement must include all of the following (Section 176.940(b)):

1. A statement of whether the journal is lost, compromised, destroyed, or stolen;

2. An explanation of how the journal became lost, compromised, destroyed, or stolen;

3. The date the Notary discovered that the journal was lost, compromised, destroyed, or stolen;

4. A statement that the journal has been destroyed or that the Notary does not possess the journal and does not know who possesses it or where it is located; and

5. A statement that, if the Notary subsequently acquires possession of the lost or stolen journal, the notary public shall file a written statement with the Secretary of State within 10 business days after the date the Notary reacquires possession of the lost or stolen journal, including a written explanation of how the journal was recovered. ■

Notary Certificate and Stamp

Notary Certificate

Requirement. In notarizing any document, a Notary must complete a Notary certificate (5 ILCS 312/6-103). The certificate is wording that indicates exactly what the Notary has certified. The Notary certificate wording may be printed either on the document itself or on an attachment to it.

The certificate must be signed and dated by the Notary and must include the state and county in which the notarial act is performed and the official seal of office (5 ILCS 312/6-103[a]).

Legible Signature. The Notary's signature must be legible. If the Notary's preferred signature is not legible and recognizable, the Notary must also legibility print the Notary's name adjacent to the signature (Section 176.600(d)).

Completing the Certificate. When filling in the blanks in the Notary certificate, Notaries should either type or print neatly in dark ink.

Correcting a Certificate. When filling out the certificate, the Notary needs to make sure any preprinted information is accurate. For example, the venue — the state and county in which the notarial act is taking place — may have been filled in prior to the notarization. If the preprinted venue is incorrect, the Notary must line through the incorrect state and/or county, write in the proper site of the notarization, and initial and date the change.

Certificate Forms. When certificate wording is not preprinted on the document, or when preprinted wording is not acceptable, the Notary may attach a certificate form. This form must be securely attached, typically by staple. The use of tape, paper clips or binder clips is not permitted (Section 176.600(c)).

If the certificate form is replacing unacceptable preprinted wording, the Notary should line through the preprinted wording and write below it, "See attached certificate." If the document has no preprinted wording, however, the Notary should not add this notation. Those words could be viewed as an unauthorized change to the document.

To prevent a certificate form from being removed and fraudulently placed on another document, the Notary may add a brief description of the document to the certificate: "This certificate is attached to a _____ (title or type of document), dated _____ (date), of _____ (number) pages, signed by _____ (name[s] of signer[s])."

The National Notary Association offers certificate forms that have similar wording preprinted on them; otherwise, the Notary will have to print, type, or stamp this information on each certificate form used. Finally, when Notaries attach a certificate form to a document, they always should note in their journals that they did so, as well as the means by which they attached the certificate to the document: "Certificate form stapled to document, following signature page."

While fraud-deterrent steps such as these can make it much more difficult for a certificate form to be removed and misused, there is no absolute protection against its removal and misuse. While a certificate form remains in their control, however, Notaries must absolutely ensure that it is attached only to its intended document.

Selecting Certificates. Non-attorney Notaries should never select Notary certificates for any transaction. It is not the role of a non-attorney Notary to decide what type of certificate — and thus what type of notarization — a document needs. As ministerial officials, Notaries generally follow instructions and complete forms that have been provided for them; they do not issue instructions or decide which forms are appropriate in a given case.

If a document is presented to a Notary without certificate wording and if the signer does not know what type of notarial act is appropriate, the signer should be asked to find out what kind of notarization and certificate are needed. Usually the agency that issued or will be accepting the document can provide this information. A Notary who selects certificates may be engaging in the unauthorized practice of law.

Do Not Pre-Sign or Pre-Seal Certificates. A Notary must never sign and/or seal certificates ahead of time or permit other persons to attach Notary certificate forms to documents. A Notary must never give or mail an unattached, signed, and sealed certificate form to another person and trust that person to attach it to a particular document, even if asked to do so by a signer who previously appeared before the Notary (INPH).

These actions could facilitate fraud or forgery, and, since such actions would be indefensible in a civil court of law, they could subject the Notary to lawsuits to recover damages resulting from the Notary's neglect or misconduct.

Notary Seal

Requirement. An Illinois Notary must use an official Notary seal to perform all notarial acts (5 ILCS 312/3-101).

Use of Official Seal. When notarizing paper documents, a legible imprint of the official seal, using a rubber stamp. must be placed on the notarial certificate at the time of the notarial act. For electronic records, the electronic seal must be attached to or logically associated with the electronic document (Section 176.500(b-c)).

The seal cannot be used for any other purpose other than performing a notarial act (Section 176.500(f)).

Seal Content. The imprint of the seal must be reasonably legible and must contain [5 ILCS 312/3-101(a)]:

- The words "Official Seal";

- The Notary's official name, printed;

- The words "Notary Public - State of Illinois";

- The words "Commission No." followed by the Notary's commission number;

- The words "My Commission Expires", followed by the Notary's commission expiration date expressed in terms of the month, one- or two-digit day, and complete year (e.g., January 1, 2024).

Seal Format. The seal must have a serrated or milled edge border in a rectangular form not more than one inch in height by two and one-half inches in length and must surround the required seal content [5 ILCS 312/3-101(a)].

Photographically Reproducible. The imprint of the official seal on paper documents must be capable of being photocopied or reproduced (Section 176.520).

Placement of the Seal Impression. The Notary's official seal should be affixed near but not over the Notary's signature on the Notary certificate.

The Notary must not place an imprint of the seal over a signature in a document or over any writing in a notarial certificate (Section 176.500(d). If there is no room for a seal, the Notary may have no choice but to complete and attach a certificate form that duplicates the notarial wording on the document.

Additional Seal Imprint. When the notarial certificate is on a separate piece of paper attached to the document, or when there are attachments to the paper document to be notarized, a Notary may use one additional imprint of the seal if the imprint does not make any part of the document illegible. The additional seal must be partially stamped together on the certificate and on the signature page or attachment to the notarized document (Section 176.500(e)).

L.S. On many certificates the letters "L.S." appear, indicating where the seal is to be located. These letters abbreviate the Latin term *locus sigilli*, meaning "place of the seal." A black inking rubber stamp seal should be placed near but not over the letters, so that wording imprinted by the seal will not be obscured.

Illegible Seal. If an initial stamp seal impression is unreadable and there is ample room on the document, another impression can be affixed nearby. Application of a second seal must not make any portion of the document unreadable. The illegibility of the first impression will indicate why a second stamp seal impression was necessary. The Notary should then record in the journal that a second impression was applied.

A Notary should never attempt to fix an imperfect stamp seal impression with pen, ink or correction fluid. This may be viewed as evidence of tampering and cause the document to be rejected by a receiving agency.

Lost, Compromised, Destroyed or Stolen Seal. If a seal is lost or stolen, the Notary must notify the Department in writing the next business day after discovering the seal was lost or stolen.

A replacement seal must contain a distinct difference from the original seal.

If the lost or stolen seal is found or recovered after a replacement has been obtained, the original seal must be destroyed (Section 176.530(a-c)).

Never Surrender Seal. The Notary's seal is the personal property of the Notary, regardless of who paid for it. The seal should never be surrendered to an employer upon termination of employment.

No person may unlawfully possess, obtain, conceal, damage or destroy this official tool of the Notary's office (5 ILCS 312/7-107). ∎

Remote and Electronic Notarization

Remote vs. Electronic Distinction

In Illinois, a "remote" notarization is performed on paper documents. Any Illinois Notary may perform such remote notarizations (AC 176.300 b). To perform "electronic" notarizations a Notary must obtain an Electronic Notary commission.

In this chapter we will discuss the following three methods for performing remote and/or electronic notarizations:

1. Notarizing paper documents for remotely located signers;

2. Notarizing electronic documents for remotely located signers; and

3. Notarizing electronic documents for signers who appear in-person.

NOTARIZING PAPER DOCUMENTS FOR REMOTELY LOCATED SIGNERS

Purpose

When a signer needing a paper document notarized cannot meet in the same physical location as the Notary, a remote notarization can be performed.

Registration

No Additional Registration Required. Any commissioned Notary in the State of Illinois has the authority to notarize paper documents for remotely located signers. No additional registration is required; keeping in mind, this applies to remote notarization of paper documents only (5 ILCS 312/2-102). A separate commission is required to notarize electronic documents (see Registration Requirements, page 54).

Bond

Additional Bond Required. Although no additional registration is required to notarize paper documents for remotely located signers, Notaries who plan to perform notarizations remotely must submit an additional $25,000 bond (5 ILCS 312/2-105).

Personal Appearance

Required. The signer appears before the Notary via two-way audio-visual communication technology that allows the signer and the Notary to engage in direct, contemporaneous interaction. The signer must attest to being physically located in Illinois and the Notary and the principal must agree to the performance of the act using audio-video communication at the outset of the notarization and before the identity of the principal has been confirmed.

Identifying the Signer

Identification. The Notary verifies the identity of the signer by either personal knowledge, the remote presentation of an acceptable identification document (see Acceptable Identification Documents, page 10), or the oath or affirmation of a credible witness. If the Notary cannot determine the identification document presented is valid, nor match the physical features on the ID presented with the signer, the Notary cannot complete the notarization using that credential (Section 176.700(b)) and (5 ILCS 312/6-102.5(a)(3).

Reviewing the Document

Requirements. During recording, the signer must specify what document is being signed. Each page of the document must be shown in a means clearly legible to the Notary, and the signing of the document must be captured up-close for the Notary to observe (Section 176.710).

Restarting the Remote Performance

Requirements. The Notary must restart the entire notarial process, including identifying the signer, if at any time during the process (Section 176.720):

1. The signer or the Notary exits the session;

2. The audio-video communication link is broken; or

3. The Notary believes the process has been compromised and cannot be completed for any reason, including poor resolution or quality of the audio or video.

Transmitting the Document

Requirements. The signer must transmit by overnight mail, fax or other electronic means the signed document no later than the day after the document is signed. The Notary then completes the notarial certificate on the transmitted copy of the document and returns the notarized copy of the document to the signer within 24 hours. If necessary, the Notary may sign the document as of the date of the original execution provided the Notary receives both the original signed document together with the electronically witnessed copy within 30 days after the date of the remotely recorded personal appearance (5 ILCS 312/6-102.5).

Audio-Video Communication Technology

Requirements. Communication technology must meet state standards and provide for synchronous audio-video sufficient to enable the Notary and remotely located principal to see and speak with each other. The process must provide a means for the remote Notary to reasonably confirm that a document is the same document in which the principal made a statement or signed. The Notary must ensure that the communication technology is sufficient to prevent the act and the recording, and any personally identifiable information disclosed during the remote notarial act from unauthorized access (Section 176.700).

Request for Recording

Available Upon Request. The recording of a remote notarial act must be made available upon request to the following persons or entities (Section 176.710(d):

1. To the principal for whom the remote notarial act was performed;

2. To the Secretary of State;

3. To a law enforcement or federal, state, or local governmental agency in the course of an enforcement action or the performance of any lawful duty;

4. Pursuant to a court order or subpoena;

5. To the Notary who performed the remote notarial act;

6. To the employer of the Notary to ensure compliance with this Part or the Act; or

7. To any other person who is authorized to obtain the recording.

Certificate Wording for Remote Notarial Acts

Certificate Wording. Illinois provides the following examples of acceptable notarial certificate wording for remote notarial acts (Section 176.730):

- For an acknowledgment in an individual capacity:

  State of Illinois

  County of _____

The foregoing instrument was acknowledged before me using audio-video technology on (date) _____ by _____ (name(s) of individual(s)) _____.

(Signature of notary public)

Notary Public

(Notary seal)

(My commission expires: _____)

- ## For an acknowledgment in a representative capacity:

State of Illinois

County of _____

The foregoing instrument was acknowledged before me using audio-video technology on (date) _____ by _____ (name(s) of individual(s)) _____ as (type of authority, such as officer or trustee) of (name of party on behalf of whom the instrument was executed).

(Signature of notary public)

Notary Public

(Notary seal)

(My commission expires: _____)

- ## For a verification on oath or affirmation:

State of Illinois

County of _____

Signed and sworn to (or affirmed) before me using audio-video technology on (date) _____ by _____ (name(s) of individual(s)) _____ making statement).

(Signature of notary public)

Notary public

(Notary seal)

(My commission expires: _____)

NOTARIZING ELECTRONIC DOCUMENTS FOR REMOTELY LOCATED SIGNERS

Purpose

When the Notary and signer cannot meet face-to-face in the same room, an electronic document can be notarized remotely. Electronic notarizations performed for remotely located signers have the same force and effect as a notarial act performed in the physical presence of a Notary.

Registration

Requirements. In order to perform electronic notarizations using audio-video communication, the person must have a traditional Notary commission in effect and an application for an electronic Notary commission must be filed with the Secretary of State (Section 176.800). In addition, the applicant must provide the name of all electronic notarization system providers the applicant intends to use to perform electronic notarial acts. A Notary may not perform electronic notarial acts until the Secretary of State has approved the application and the registration of the electronic notarization system provider(s).

Bond

Additional Bond Required. Notaries who perform notarizations either remotely or electronically and by means of audio-video communication are required to obtain and maintain a surety bond in the amount of $25,000 in addition to the $5,000 bond required for traditional Notaries (5 ILCS 312/2-105).

Procedure

Requirements. Notarizing electronic documents for remotely located signers requires the Notary and signer to meet via audio-video technology that allows them to see and hear each other in real-time. The electronic record or document and the electronic Notary certificate are uploaded to a shared platform by a state approved Notary technology provider, and the notarization takes place via that platform. The Notary would still follow the fundamental steps for the notarization. The Notary screens the signer for identity, willingness and awareness and certifies the facts for the requested notarization. Then the Notary completes the electronic certificate and affixes an electronic signature and seal. A journal record is made, along with an audio-video recording of the transaction.

Personal Appearance

Required. The signer appears before the Notary via two-way audio-visual communication technology that allows the signer and the Notary to engage in direct, contemporaneous interaction.

Location. The Notary must be located within the state of Illinois at the time of the remote online notarization. However, the signer is not required to be within the state of Illinois at the time of notarization. The signer can be located within the state of Illinois, outside of Illinois but within the United States, or outside the United States if the document is to be filed with or relates to a matter before a public official or court, governmental entity, or other entity subject to the jurisdiction of the United States or involves property located in the United States or involves a transaction substantially connected with the United States (5 ILCS 312/3-105(b-c)).

Venue. During the recording, the Notary must identify the venue for the notarization as the jurisdiction within Illinois where the Notary is physically located at the time of notarization.

Agreement. The Notary and the principal must agree to the performance of the act using audio-video communication at the outset of the notarization and before the identity of the principal has been confirmed (Section 176.860 9(a).

Identifying Document Signers

Requirements. Verifying the signer's identity remains one of the most important roles of the Notary. The identity of the principal must be confirmed by the following (Section 176.860 9(b):

1. Personal knowledge;

2. The oath of a credible witness who personally knows the principal and the Notary; or each of the following:

   A. Remote presentation by the person of a government-issued identification credential that contains a photograph and the signature of the person;

   B. Credential analysis of the government-issued credential, typically provided by the electronic Notary system provider (see Credential Analysis, see page 56); and

   C. A dynamic knowledge-based authentication assessment that satisfies state requirements or identity proofing in accordance with state regulations. This option is provided by the electronic Notary system provider (see Identity Proofing below).

Credential Analysis. Credential Analysis is a procedure that analyzes the principal's identification credential presented remotely against trusted third-person data sources using automated software processes to confirm the identification document is not fraudulent or modified and enables the Notary to visually compare the information and photograph and the principal (Section 176.835(a-b)).

Identity Proofing — Knowledge Based Assessment. Identity Proofing is performed using a dynamic knowledge-based authentication assessment. The principal must answer a quiz consisting of a minimum of five questions related to the principal's personal history or identity formulated from public or private data sources (Section 176.835(c).

Unable to Confirm. If the Notary cannot determine that an ID presented by the principal is valid or cannot match the physical features of the principal with the credential presented, the Notary must not take any further action to complete the act by using that credential.

Recording Identification Information. If the signer is identified by personal knowledge, the recording must include an explanation by the Notary as to how he or she knows the signer and how long he or she has known the signer. If the person for whom the electronic notarial act is being performed is identified by a credible witness, the credible witness must appear before the electronic Notary; and the recording of the electronic notarial act must include:

A.   A statement by the Notary as to whether he or she identified the credible witness by personal knowledge or satisfactory evidence; and

B.   An explanation by the credible witness as to how he or she knows the signer and how long he or she has known the signer (5 ILCS 312/6A-104).

Reviewing the Document

Requirements. During the recording the Notary must be satisfied that the document presented for notarization is the same document being signed by the Notary (5 ILCS 312/6A-104(f)(3)).

Restarting the Remote Performance

Requirements. When notarizing electronic documents remotely, a Notary must restart the performance of the remote notarial act from the beginning, including confirming the identity of the principal under the following circumstances (Section 176.860):

•   The principal or the remotely located Notary exits the session;

•   The audio-video communication link is broken; or

•   The remotely located Notary believes that the process of completing the remote notarial act has been compromised and cannot be completed because of the resolution or quality of the audio or video transmission, or both.

Single Recorded Session. The entire notarization process must be recorded in a single recorded session.

Electronic Notarial Certificate

Notarial Certificate Required. As with traditional notarizations, the Notary must compete a notarial certificate for each transaction. When completing a Notary certificate for a remote online notarization, the certificate must indicate that the notarization was performed using audio-video communication technology and the Notary must affix a tamper-evident electronic signature and seal to the Notary certificate.

Illinois provides the following examples of acceptable notarial certificate wording for electronic notarizations (Section 176.865):

- For an acknowledgment in an individual capacity:

  State of Illinois

  County of _____

  The foregoing instrument was acknowledged before me using an electronic notarization system provider on _____ (date) by _____ (name(s) of individual(s)).

  (Signature of notary public)

  Notary Public

  (Electronic seal)

  (My commission expires:)

- For an acknowledgment in a representative capacity:

  State of Illinois

  County of _____

  The foregoing instrument was acknowledged before me using an electronic notarization system provider on _____ (date) by _____ (name(s) of individual(s)) as _____ (type of authority, such as officer or trustee) of _____ (name of party on behalf of whom the instrument was executed).

  (Signature of notary public)

Notary Public

(Electronic seal)

(My commission expires:)

- ## For a verification on oath or affirmation:

State of Illinois

County of _____

Signed and sworn to (or affirmed) before me using an electronic notarization system provider on _____ (date) by _____ (name(s) of individual(s) making statement).

(Signature of notary public)

Notary public

(Electronic seal)

(My commission expires:)

- ## For witnessing or attesting a signature:

State of Illinois

County of _____

Signed or attested before me on _____ (date) by _____ (name(s) of persons(s))

(Signature of notary Public)

(Electronic seal)

(My commission expires:)

Electronic Seal and Electronic Signature

Electronic Seal and Electronic Signature

Required. Electronic Notaries must maintain an electronic seal and at least one digital certificate that includes the Notary's electronic signature.

Electronic Seal Description. The electronic seal must look identical to a traditional Notary seal (see Description of Seal, page

46), be accompanied by the electronic signature of the Notary and must include language explicitly stating that the electronic notarial act was performed using audio-video commination, if applicable (5 ILCS 312/3-101(b-5).

Access and Use of Electronic Notary Seal and Electronic Signature. An electronic Notary's signature and seal can only be used by the Notary to whom it is registered and must be protected using a biometric authentication, password authentication, token authentication, or other form of authentication approved by the Secretary (Sec. 176.815(b)).

Report of Theft or Vandalism. An electronic Notary must report in writing to the Secretary the theft or vandalism of the Notary's electronic signature or electronic seal no later than the next business day after discovering the theft or vandalism. Failure to report the theft or vandalism is grounds for commission revocation (Sec. 176.815(b)).

Replacing an Electronic Seal or Digital Certificate. An electronic Notary must replace an electronic seal or digital certificate under the following circumstances:

- The electronic seal or certificate has expired;

- The electronic seal or certificate has been revoked or terminated by the device's issuing or registering authority; or

- The electronic seal or certificate is no longer valid or capable of authentication (Section 176.820(c).

Notification of Replacing an Electronic Seal or Digital Certificate. A Notary who replaces an electronic seal or digital certificate must provide the following to the Secretary of State within 10 days after the replacement:

- The electronic technology or technologies to be used in attaching or logically associating the new electronic seal or digital certificate to an electronic document;

- The electronic Notary's new digital certificate, if applicable;

- A copy of the electronic Notary's new electronic seal, if applicable; and

- Any necessary instructions or techniques supplied by the vendor that allow the electronic Notary's electronic seal or digital certificate to be read and authenticated (Section 176.820(c).

Journal and Audio-Video Recording

Required. Electronic Notaries must keep, maintain and keep secure a journal entry of all remote online notarizations performed. In addition to the journal, an audio video recording of the entire remote online notarization must be made.

Journal Exception. A Notary employed by an attorney or law firm is not required to keep a journal during of the Notary's employment if the attorney or law firm maintains a copy of the documents notarized. No attorney or law firm is required to violate attorney-client privilege by allowing or authorizing inspection of any notarizations that are recorded in a Notary's journal. Journals of notarizations performed solely within the course of a Notary's employment with an attorney or law firm is the property of the employing attorney or firm (Section 176.900).

Required Journal Entries. Each journal entry must contain specific information (see Required Journal Entries, page 38).

Prohibited Journal Entries. Illinois Notaries are prohibited from recording specific personal information in the journal (see Prohibited Journal Entries, page 39).

Retention and Storing Electronic Journals and Recordings. A Notary may use a system provider to store the electronic journal and recording if the provider has registered with the Secretary of State and the provider's certification is in effect. The provider must allow the Notary sole control of the electronic journal and the recording. The journal and audio-visual recording must be maintained for at least seven years and must be made available to the Secretary of State upon request.

Retention Requirement Exception. Retention requirements do not apply to Notaries in the course of their employment with a governmental entity (IAC 176.960 f)).

Backup. Notaries must take reasonable steps to ensure that a backup of the electronic journal and audio-visual recording exists and is secure from unauthorized use.

Journal and Audio-Video Inspection. Because a journal is a public record, members of the public can inspect a journal entry (see Journal Inspection, page 42). The same provisions that apply to journal inspections apply to audio-video inspections.

Subpoenas and Investigative Requests. A request for inspection of a journal or audio-video recording made through an investigative request by law enforcement or by the Secretary of State or in a subpoena must be complied with in the manner specified in the request or subpoena.

Confidential Information. If any portion of the audio-video recording of an electronic or remote notarization includes biometric information or includes an image of the identification card, that portion of the recording is confidential and must not be released without consent of the individual whose identity is being established, unless ordered by a court of competent jurisdiction or upon request by the Secretary of State.

Lost, Compromised, Destroyed or Stolen Journal. If a Notary's journal is lost, compromised, destroyed or stolen the Notary must notify the Secretary of State in writing or electronically the next business day after discovery (see Lost, Stolen or Compromised Journal, page 42). The provisions that apply for lost, compromised, destroyed or stolen journals also apply to audio-video recordings.

Death or Adjudication of Incompetency of a Notary. Upon the death or adjudication of incompetency of a current or former Notary, the Notary's personal representative or guardian or any other person knowingly in possession of an electronic journal or audio-visual recording must:

- Comply with the 7-year retention requirements (See Retention and Storing Electronic Journals and Recordings, page 61). Retention requirements do not apply to Notaries employed with a governmental entity.

- Transmit the journal and recording to one or more depositories (Section 176.960).

- Transmit the journal and recording in an industry-standard readable data storage device to the Illinois Secretary of State, Index Department at 111 E. Monroe St., Springfield, IL 62756.

Communication Technology

Standards. Communication technology must meet the following standards (Section 176.825):

- Provide synchronous audio-video feeds of sufficient video resolution and audio clarity to enable the electronic Notary and the individual to see and speak with each other in real time. The process must provide a means for the electronic Notary reasonably to confirm that an electronic record before the electronic Notary is the same record in which the individual made a statement or on which the individual executed a signature.

- Provide reasonable security measures to prevent unauthorized access to:

1. The live transmission of the audio-video feeds;

2. The methods used to perform identity verification;

3. The electronic record that is the subject of the electronic notarization; and

4. Any electronic Notary's journal or audio-video recordings maintained or stored as a function of the communication technology

NOTARIZING ELECTRONIC DOCUMENTS FOR SIGNERS WHO APPEAR IN-PERSON (IPEN)

Procedure

Requirements. In-person electronic notarization still requires the Notary and signer to meet face-to-face and be physically in the same room. Like pen and paper notarizations, the Notary must identify the signer through personal knowledge or satisfactory evidence, screen the signer for willingness and awareness, and certify the facts for the requested notarization. However, for electronic notarizations, the document is presented electronically, such as on a computer or tablet, and the signature will be affixed electronically by the signer. The Notary certificate will be provided at the end of the document or logically attached to the document for the Notary to complete and affix the electronic signature and seal. And just like with a paper notarization, a journal entry is required.

At the time of this publication, the Illinois Compiled Statutes and administrative rules do not prescribe rules explicitly for in-person electronic notarial acts. However, the Illinois Secretary of State has informed the National Notary Association that Notaries wanting to perform in-person electronic notarial acts must be commissioned as an Illinois Electronic Notary and Electronic Notaries may only use approved platforms.

Fees for Electronic Notary Services

Fees. A Notary may charge up to $25 for each electronic notarization. ■

Misconduct, Fines and Penalties

Misconduct

Definition. Official misconduct generally means the wrongful exercise of a power or the wrongful performance of a duty. It is fully defined in Section 33-3 of the Criminal Code of 2012 [720 ILCS 5/33-3].

Incomplete Documents. A Notary may not notarize a blank or incomplete document (INPH).

Certificate Forms. A Notary may not sign a blank affidavit or acknowledgment certificate and deliver the signed form for use by another person (5 ILCS 312/6-104[c]).

Declared Incapacity. A Notary may not notarize the signature of a person he or she knows to have been declared mentally ill by a court unless the person has been subsequently restored to mental health as a matter of record (5 ILCS 312/6-104[d]).

Blind Signers. An Illinois Notary is prohibited from taking the acknowledgment of a person who is blind unless the Notary has first read the document to the person (5 ILCS 312/6-104[e]).

Non-English Speaking Signers. Illinois law specifically prohibits Notaries from taking the acknowledgment of anyone who does not speak or understand English unless the nature and effect of the document to be notarized is translated into a language the person does understand (5 ILCS 312/6-104[f]).

Change Documents. Notaries are not allowed to change anything in a document after it has been signed by anyone (5 ILCS 312/6-104[g]).

Unauthorized Practice of Law. Non-attorney Notaries may never prepare any legal document or fill in the blanks of a document for another person (5 ILCS 312/6-104[h]). Notaries may be prosecuted for rendering, offering to render, or holding themselves out as rendering any service constituting the unauthorized practice of law (5 ILCS 312/7-109).

Notaries who are not attorneys or accredited immigration representatives may not accept payment in exchange for providing legal advice or any other assistance that requires legal analysis, legal judgment, or interpretation of the law (5 ILCS 312/3-103[e]). Violation of this provision is a business offense punishable by a fine of three times the amount received for services (with a $1,001 minimum) and restitution of the amount paid to the Notary's customer. These fines do not preclude additional appropriate civil remedies or criminal charges available under law (5 ILCS 312/3-103[f]).

Foreign-Language Advertising. An Illinois Notary may not literally translate from English into another language terms or titles including, but not limited to, "Notary Public," "Notary," "licensed," "attorney," "lawyer" or any other term that implies that he or she is an attorney.

Further, a Notary who is not an attorney or an accredited immigration representative may not advertise in a language other than English without posting, in English and the foreign language, both a schedule of fees and a disclaimer stating:

> "I AM NOT AN ATTORNEY LICENSED TO PRACTICE LAW IN ILLINOIS. I AM NOT ALLOWED TO DRAFT LEGAL DOCUMENTS OR RECORDS, NOR MAY I GIVE LEGAL ADVICE ON ANY MATTER, INCLUDING, BUT NOT LIMITED TO, MATTERS OF IMMIGRATION, OR ACCEPT OR CHARGE FEES FOR THE PERFORMANCE OF THOSE ACTIVITIES."

Each language must be on a separate sign (815 ILCS 505/2AA/5).

A Notary who is subject to the foreign-language advertising requirement must provide to persons seeking notarial services an acknowledgment form reciting the legal notice in substantially the same form as the statement required for written and electronic advertisements, and must have the person seeking notarial services sign the form; and further provides that the Notary must provide a copy of the signed form to the person and retain a copy of the signed form throughout their current commission and for 2 years thereafter. The acknowledgment form will be translated by the Secretary of State into Spanish and any other language the Secretary deems necessary and provided on the Secretary's website.

Violations of the foreign-language advertisement provisions are punishable by a $1,500 fine for each offense and permanent revocation of the Notary's commission upon the second violation. In addition, the Notary may be subject to other civil or criminal penalties (5 ILCS 312/3-103).

Immigration Expert. Non-attorney Notaries may not represent themselves to be experts on immigration matters or provide any other assistance that requires legal analysis, legal judgment, or interpretation of the law unless they are a designated entity as defined by the Code of Federal Regulations or an entity accredited by the Board of Immigration Appeals (5 ILCS 312/3-103[c]).

Any Notary Public who violates these provisions is guilty of official misconduct and subject to fines or imprisonment. Furthermore, anyone harmed by a Notary's actions in this context may pursue other civil remedies available under the law (5 ILCS 312/3-103[d]).

Failure to Transmit Funds. Notaries must transmit or forward funds that they have taken from a person for whom they have performed a notarization and that they have accepted specifically for the purpose of transmitting or forwarding to another person (5 ILCS 312/6-104[i]).

Providing Receipts and Keeping Records of Fees. All notaries public must provide receipts and keep records for fees accepted for services provided. Failure to provide receipts and keep records that can be presented as evidence of no wrongdoing shall be construed as a presumptive admission of allegations raised in complaints against the notary for violations related to accepting prohibited fees (P.A. 85-593; 93-1001, §5; 95-988, §5; 98-29, §5).

Overcharging. If a Notary charges more than the legally prescribed fees, he or she may be guilty of a Class A misdemeanor for the first offense. If a second offense is committed within five years of the previous conviction, the Notary may be guilty of a Class 3 felony. In addition, the Attorney General or any state's attorney may bring action against the violator and civil action may be brought as well (5 ILCS 312/3-104).

Revocation

Application Misstatement or Omission. The Illinois Secretary of State may revoke the commission of any Notary who submits an application containing any substantial and material misstatement or omission of fact (5 ILCS 312/7-108[a]).

Felony or Official Misconduct. The Secretary of State may revoke the commission of any Notary found guilty of any felony or official misconduct (5 ILCS 312/7-108[b]).

Disposition of Seal. If a Notary's commission is revoked, the official Notary stamp seal should be destroyed or defaced to prevent its fraudulent use (INPH).

Disbarred Attorney. The Secretary of State may revoke the commission of a Notary who is a licensed attorney and has been sanctioned, suspended, or disbarred by the Illinois Attorney Registration and Disciplinary Commission or the Illinois Supreme Court (5 ILCS 312/7-108(3)).

Civil Liability

Liability of Notary. An Illinois Notary public and the surety on the Notary's bond are liable to the persons involved for all damages caused by the Notary's intentional or unintentional misconduct or neglect (5 ILCS 312/7-101). The $5,000 bond offers no protection to the Notary, since the Notary is required by law to reimburse the bonding firm for any funds paid out to a victim of the Notary's misconduct. A civil lawsuit against the Notary may seek financial recovery against any and all of the Notary's personal assets (5 ILCS 312/7-101).

Liability of Employer. The employer of a Notary may also be held liable for damages proximately caused by a Notary acting within the scope of his or her employment and whose notarial actions are known and permitted by the employer (5 ILCS 312/7-102).

Criminal Penalties

Official Misconduct. A Notary who knowingly and recklessly commits any official misconduct is guilty of a Class A misdemeanor (5 ILCS 312/7-105).

A Notary who negligently commits any official misconduct is guilty of a Class B misdemeanor (5 ILCS 312/7-105).

Willful Impersonation of Notary. Anyone who is not commissioned as a Notary Public in Illinois but acts as or impersonates a Notary is guilty of a Class A misdemeanor (5 ILCS 312/7-106).

Wrongful Possession of Notary Seal. A person who unlawfully possesses a Notary's official seal is guilty of a misdemeanor and subject to a fine not exceeding $1,000 (5 ILCS 312/7-107). ■

Illinois Laws Pertaining to Notaries Public

Reprinted on the following pages are the pertinent sections of the *Illinois Compiled Statutes* affecting Notaries and notarial acts.

ILLINOIS COMPILED STATUTES

CHAPTER 5. GENERAL PROVISIONS

ACT 312. ILLINOIS NOTARY PUBLIC ACT

ARTICLE I

GENERAL PROVISIONS

5 ILCS 312/1-101 Short Title

This Act may be cited as the Illinois Notary Public Act.

History

P.A. 86-1475.

5 ILCS 312/1-102 Purposes and Rules of Construction

(a) This Act shall be construed and applied to promote its underlying purposes and policies.

(b) The underlying purposes and policies of this Act are:

(1) to simplify, clarify, and modernize the law governing notaries public; and

(2) to promote, serve, and protect the public interest.

History

P.A. 84-322.

5 ILCS 312/1-103 Prospective Effect of Act

This Act applies prospectively. Nothing in this Act shall be construed to revoke any notary public commission existing on the effective date of this Act. All reappointments of notarial commissions shall be obtained in accordance with this Act.

History

P.A. 84-322.

5 ILCS 312/1-104 Definitions.

As used in this Act:

"Accredited immigration representative" means a not for profit organization recognized by the Board of Immigration Appeals under 8 C.F.R. 292.29(a) and employees of those organizations accredited under 8 C.F.R. 292.29(d).

"Acknowledgment" means a declaration by an individual before a notarial officer that the individual has signed a record for the purpose stated in the record and, if the record is signed in a representative capacity, that the individual signed the record with proper authority and signed it as the act of the individual or entity identified in the record.

"Audio-video communication" means communication by which a person is able to see, hear, and communicate with another person in real time using electronic means.

"Communication technology" means an electronic device or process that allows a notary public and a remotely located individual to communicate with each other simultaneously by audio-video communication.

"Credential" means a tangible record evidencing the identity of a person, including a valid and unexpired identification card or other document issued by the federal government or any state government that contains the photograph and signature of the principal.

"Digital certificate" means a computer-based record or electronic file to a notary public or applicant for commission as an electronic notary public for the purpose of creating an official electronic signature. The digital certificate shall be kept in the exclusive control of the electronic notary public.

"Dynamic knowledge based authentication assessment" means an identity assessment that is based on a set of questions formulated from public or private data sources for which the person taking the assessment has not previously provided an answer that meets any rules adopted by the Secretary of State.

"Electronic" means of or relating to technology having electrical, digital, magnetic, wireless, optical, electromagnetic, or similar capabilities.

"Electronic document" means information that is created, generated, sent, communicated, received, or stored by electronic means.

"Electronic notarial act" means an act that an electronic notary public of this State is authorized to perform. The term includes:

(1) taking an acknowledgment;

(2) administering an oath or affirmation;

(3) executing a jurat;

(4) certifying a true and correct copy; and

(5) performing such other duties as may be prescribed by a specific statute.

"Electronic notarial certificate" means the portion of a notarized electronic document that is completed by an online notary public and contains the following:

(1) the electronic notary public's electronic signature, electronic seal, title, and commission expiration date;

(2) other required information concerning the date and placement of the electronic notarization; and

(3) the facts attested to or certified by the electronic notary public in the particular notarization.

"Electronic notarial certificate" includes the form of an acknowledgment, jurat, verification on oath or affirmation, or verification of witness or attestation that is completed remotely by an electronic notary public and:

(1) contains the electronic notary's electronic signature, electronic seal, title and commission, and expiration date;

(2) contains other required information concerning the date and place of the electronic notarization;

(3) otherwise conforms to the requirements for an acknowledgment, jurat, verification on oath or affirmation, or verification of witness or attestation under the laws of this State; and

(4) indicates that the person making the acknowledgment, oath, or affirmation appeared.

"Electronic notarization system" means a set of applications, programs, hardware, software, or technology to enable an electronic notary to perform electronic notarial acts through audiovideo communication.

"Electronic notary public" means a person commissioned by the Secretary of State to perform electronic notarial acts.

"Electronic presentation" means the transmission of a quality image of a government-issued identification credential to an electronic notary public through communication technology for the purpose of enabling the electronic notary public to identify the person appearing before the electronic notary public and to perform a credential analysis.

"Electronic record" means a record created, generated, sent, communicated, received, or stored by electronic means.

"Electronic seal" means information within a notarized electronic document that includes the names, commission number, jurisdiction, and expiration date of the commission of an electronic notary public and generally includes the information required to be set forth in a mechanical stamp under subsection (b-5) of Section 3-101 [5 ILCS 312/3-101].

"Electronic signature" means the official signature of the commissioned notary that is on file with the Secretary of State and has been reduced to an electronic format that may be attached to or logically associated with a record and executed or adopted by an individual with the intent to sign the record.

"Identity proofing" means a process or service operating according to criteria approved by the Secretary of state through which a third person affirms the identity of an individual through review of personal information from public and proprietary data sources, including (a) by means of dynamic knowledge-based authentication, such as a review of personal information from public or proprietary data sources; or (b) by means of analysis of biometric data, such as, but not limited to, facial recognition, voiceprint analysis, or fingerprint analysis.

"In the presence of" or "appear before" means:

(1) being in the same physical location as another person and close enough to see, hear, communicate with and exchange credentials with that person; or

(2) being in a different physical location from another person, but able to see, hear, and communicate with the person by means of audio-video communication that meets any rules adopted by the Secretary of State.

"Notarial act" means an act, whether performed with respect to a tangible or electronic record, that a notary public, a remote notary public, or an electronic notary public may perform under the laws of this State. "Notary act" includes taking an acknowledgment, administering an oath, or affirmation, taking a verification on oath, or affirmation, witnessing or attesting a signature, certifying or attesting a copy, and noting a protest of a negotiable instrument.

"Notary public" or "notary" means an individual commissioned to perform notarial acts.

"Notarization" means the performance of a notarial act.

"Outside the United States" means a location outside of the geographic boundaries of a state or commonwealth of the United States, the District of Columbia, Puerto Rico, the United States Virgin Islands, and any territory, or insular possession, or other location subject to the jurisdiction of the United States.

"Principal" means an individual:

(1) whose signature is notarized; or

(2) taking an oath or affirmation from the notary but not in the capacity of a witness for the notarization.

"Public key certificate" means an electronic credential which is used to identify an individual who signed an electronic record with the certificate.

"Real time" means the actual span of uninterrupted time during which all parts of an electronic notarial act occur.

"Remote notarial act" means a notarial act that is done by way of audio-video communication technology that allows for direct, contemporaneous interaction between the individual signing the document (the signatory) and the witness by sight and sound but that requires the notary public to use his or her physical stamp and seal to notarize the document without the aid of an electronic seal or signature.

"Remote notary public" means any notary public that performs a remote notarial act.

"Tamper evident" means that any change to an electronic document shall display evidence of the change.

"Unique to the electronic notary public" and "sole control" mean, with respect to an electronic notarization that the signing device used to affix the electronic signature of the electronic notary public and to render the official electronic seal information tamper evident must be accessible by and attributable solely to the electronic notary public to the exclusion of all other persons and entities for the necessary period of time that such device is engaged and operating to effectuate the authorized electronic notarization.

5 ILCS 312/1-105 Notarization Task Force on Best Practices and Verification Standards to Implement Electronic Notarization. [Repealed]

2017 P.A. 100-440, § 5, effective July 1, 2017; 2020 P.A. 101-645, § 5, effective June 26, 2020; repealed internally by P.A. 101-645, § 5, effective July 1, 2021.

5 ILCS 312/1-106 Electronic Notarization Fund.

The Electronic Notarization Fund is created as a special fund in the State treasury. Moneys in the Electronic Notarization Fund during the preceding calendar year, shall be distributed, subject to appropriation, to the Secretary of State to fund the Department of Index's implementation and maintenance of the electronic notarization commissions. This Section is effective on and after July 1, 2022.

History

2021 P.A. 102-160, § 5, effective January 1, 2022.

ARTICLE II

APPOINTMENT PROVISIONS

5 ILCS 312/2-101 Appointment.

(a) The Secretary of State may appoint and commission as notaries public for a 4-year term as many persons resident in a county in this State as he deems necessary. The Secretary of State may appoint and commission as notaries public for a one-year term as many persons who are residents of a state bordering Illinois whose place of work or business is within a county in this State as the Secretary deems necessary, but only if the laws of that state authorize residents of Illinois to be appointed and commissioned as notaries public in that state.

(b) A notary public commissioned in this State may apply for an electronic notary public commission to perform electronic notarial acts with the name that appears on the notary's commission.

(c) An individual may apply for a notary public commission and apply for an electronic notary public commission at the same time.

(d) Any notary or electronic notary appointed by the Secretary of State may elect not to perform a notarial act or an electronic notarial act for any reason.

(e) The commission of a notary public and an electronic notary public shall have the same term pursuant to subsection (a).

(f) The electronic notary public commission of a notary public is suspended by operation of law when the notary public is no longer appointed and commissioned as a notary public in this State under this Act. If the commission of the notary public has been revoked or suspended, the Secretary of State shall immediately notify the notary public in writing that his or her commission as a notary public and as an electronic notary public will be suspended by operation of law until he or she is reappointed.

History

P.A. 84-322; 91-818, § 5; contingently amended by 2021 P.A. 102-160, § 5, effective January 1, 2022.

5 ILCS 312/2-101.5 Course of study and examination.

(a) Applicants applying for the first time as a notary public or as an electronic notary public or applying to renew his or her appointment as a notary public or as an electronic notary public shall:

(1) complete any course of study on notarization and electronic notarization that is required by the Secretary of State; and

(2) pass an examination at the completion of the course.

(b) The Secretary of State shall have the authority to adopt administrative rules mandating a course of study and examination and establishing the course of study content, length of the course of study to be required, and to approve any course of study providers.

History

Contingently enacted by 2021 P.A. 102-160, § 5, effective January 1, 2022.

5 ILCS 312/2-102 Application.

(a) Application for notary public commission. Every applicant for appointment and commission as a notary shall complete an application in a format prescribed by the Secretary of State to be filed with the Secretary of State, stating:

(1) the applicant's official name, as it appears on his or her current driver's license or stateissued identification card;

(2) the county in which the applicant resides or, if the applicant is a resident of a state bordering Illinois, the county in Illinois in which that person's principal place of work or principal place of business is located;

(3) the applicant's residence address, as it appears on his or her current driver's license or state-issued identification card;

(4) the applicant's e-mail address;

(5) the applicant's business address if different than the applicant's residence address, if performing notarial acts constitutes any portion of the applicant's job duties;

(6) that the applicant has resided in the State of Illinois for 30 days preceding the application or that the applicant who is a resident of a state bordering Illinois has worked or maintained a business in Illinois for 30 days preceding the application;

(7) that the applicant is a citizen of the United States or lawfully admitted for permanent residence in the United States;

(8) the applicant's date of birth;

(9) that the applicant is proficient in English language;

(10) that the applicant has not had a prior application or commission revoked due to a finding or decision by the Secretary of State;

(11) that the applicant has not been convicted of a felony;

(12) that the applicant's signature authorizes the Office of the Secretary of State to conduct a verification to confirm the information provided in the application, including a criminal background check of the applicant, if necessary;

(13) that the applicant has provided satisfactory proof to the Secretary of State that the applicant has successfully completed any required course of study on notarization; and

(14) any other information the Secretary of State deems necessary.

(b) Any notary appointed under subsection (a) shall have the authority to conduct remote notarizations.

(c) Application for electronic notary public commission. An application for an electronic notary public commission must be filed with the Secretary of State in a manner prescribed by the Secretary of State. Every applicant for appointment and commission as an electronic notary public shall complete an application to be filed with the Secretary of State, stating:

(1) all information required to be included in an application for appointment as an electronic notary public, as provided under subsection (a);

(2) that the applicant is commissioned as a notary public under this Act;

(3) the applicant's email address;

(4) that the applicant has provided satisfactory proof to the Secretary of State that the applicant has successfully completed any required course of study on electronic notarization and passed a qualifying examination;

(5) a description of the technology or device that the applicant intends to use to create his or her electronic signature in performing electronic notarial acts;

(6) the electronic signature of the applicant; and

(7) any other information the Secretary of State deems necessary.

(d) Electronic notarial acts. Before an electronic notary public performs an electronic notarial act using audio-video communication, he or she must be granted an electronic notary public commission by the Secretary of State under this Section, and identify the technology that the electronic notary public intends to use, which must be approved by the Secretary of State.

(e) Approval of commission. Upon the applicant's fulfillment of the requirements for a notarial commission or an electronic notary public commission, the Secretary of State shall approve the commission and issue to the applicant a unique commission number.

(f) Rejection of application. The Secretary of State may reject an application for a notarial commission or an electronic notary public commission if the applicant fails to comply with any Section of this Act.

History

P.A. 85-593; 91-818, § 5; 93-1001, § 5; 99-112, § 5; 2018 P.A. 100-809, § 5, effective January 1, 2019; 2021 P.A. 102-160, § 5, effective January 1, 2022; 2022 P.A. 102-160, § 5, effective May 27, 2022; 2022 P.A. 102-1030, § 5, effective May 27, 2022.

5 ILCS 312/2-102.5 Online application system.

(a) The Secretary of State may establish and maintain an online application system that permits an Illinois resident to apply for appointment and commission as a notary public or electronic notary public.

(b) Any such online application system shall employ security measures to ensure the accuracy and integrity of notary public applications submitted electronically under this Section.

(c) The Secretary of State may cross reference information provided by applicants with that contained in the Secretary of State's driver's license and Illinois Identification Card databases in order to match the information submitted by applicants, and may receive from those databases the applicant's digitized signature upon a successful match of the applicant's information with that information contained in the databases.

(d) An online application shall contain all of the information that is required for a paper application as provided in Section 2-102 of this Act [5 ILCS 312/2-102]. The applicant shall also be required to provide:

(1) the applicant's full Illinois driver's license or Illinois Identification Card number;

(2) the date of issuance of the Illinois driver's license or Illinois Identification Card; and

(3) the applicant's e-mail address for notices to be provided under this Section.

(e) For his or her application to be accepted, the applicant shall mark the box associated with the following statement included as part of the online application: By clicking on the box below, I swear or affirm all of the following:

(1) I am the person whose name and identifying information is provided on this form, and I desire to be appointed and commissioned as a notary public in the State of Illinois.

(2) All the information I have provided on this form is true and correct as of the date I am submitting this form.

(3) I authorize the Secretary of State to utilize my signature on file with the Secretary of State driver's license and Illinois Identification Card databases and understand that such signature will be used on this online application for appointment and commission as a notary public or electronic notary as if I had signed this form personally.

(4) I authorize the Secretary of State to utilize my signature to conduct a verification to confirm the information provided in the application, including a criminal background check, if necessary.

(f) Immediately upon receiving a completed online application, the online system shall send by electronic mail a confirmation notice that the application has been received. Upon completion of the procedure outlined in subsection (c) of this Section, the online application system shall send by electronic mail a notice informing the applicant of whether the following information has been matched with the Secretary of State driver's license and Illinois Identification Card databases:

(1) that the applicant has an authentic Illinois driver's license or Illinois Identification Card issued by the Secretary of State and that the driver's license or Illinois Identification Card number provided by the applicant matches the driver's license or Illinois Identification Card number for that person on file with the Secretary of State;

(2) that the date of issuance of the Illinois driver's license or Illinois Identification Card listed on the application matches the date of issuance of that license or card for that person on file with the Secretary of State;

(3) that the date of birth provided by the applicant matches the date of birth for that person on file with the Secretary of State;

(4) that the residence address provided by the applicant matches the residence address for that person on file with the Secretary of State; and

(5) the last 4 digits of the applicant's social security number.

(g) If the information provided by the applicant matches all of the criteria identified in subsection (f) of this Section, the online application system shall retrieve from the Secretary of State's database files an electronic copy of the applicant's signature from his or her Illinois driver's license or Illinois Identification Card and such signature shall be deemed to be the applicant's signature on his or her online application.

History

Contingently enacted by 2015 P.A. 99-112, § 5, effective January 1, 2016; contingently amended by 2021 P.A. 102-160, § 5, effective January 1, 2022.

5 ILCS 312/2-103 Appointment Fee.

(a) Every applicant for appointment and commission as a notary public shall pay to the Secretary of State a fee of $15. Ten dollars from each applicant fee shall be deposited in the General Revenue Fund. Five dollars from each applicant fee shall be deposited in the Electronic Notarization Fund.

(b) Every applicant for a commission as an electronic notary public shall pay to the Secretary of State a fee of $25. This fee is in addition to the fee proscribed for a commission as a notary public and shall be deposited in the Electronic Notarization Fund.

(c) The changes made to this Section by this amendatory Act of the 102nd General Assembly are effective on and after July 1, 2022.

History

P.A. 85-1396; 2021 P.A. 102-160, § 5, effective July 1, 2022.

5 ILCS 312/2-104 Oath.

(a) Every applicant for appointment and commission as a notary public shall take the following oath:

> "I, (name of applicant), solemnly affirm, under the penalty of perjury, that the answers to all questions in this application are true, complete, and correct; that I have carefully read the notary law of this State; and that, if appointed and commissioned as a notary public, I will perform faithfully, to the best of my ability, all notarial acts in accordance with the law.".

(b) In the event that the applicant completes a paper application for appointment and commission as a notary public, he or she shall take the oath in the presence of a person qualified to administer an oath in this State. The printed oath shall be followed by the signature of the applicant and notarized as follows:

> "_____ (Signature of applicant)
> State of Illinois
>
> County of (name of county where the notarization is completed)
> Subscribed and affirmed before me on (insert date) by (name of person whose signature is being notarized).
>
> (Official signature and official seal of notary)"

(c) In the event that the applicant completes an online application for appointment and commission as a notary public, he or she shall affirm the oath electronically. An electronic affirmation of the oath in the online application system shall have the same force and effect as an oath sworn and affirmed in person.

History

P.A. 84-322; 91-357, § 8; 99-112, § 5; contingently amended by 2021 P.A. 102-160, § 5, effective January 1, 2022.

5 ILCS 312/2-105 Bond.

(a) Every application for appointment and commission as a notary public shall be accompanied by or logically associated with an executed bond commencing on the date of the appointment with a term of 4 years, in the sum of $5,000, with, as surety thereon, a company qualified to write surety bonds in this State. The bond shall be conditioned upon the faithful performance of all notarial acts in accordance with this Act. The Secretary of State may prescribe an official bond form.

(b) A notary public that performs notarizations either remotely or electronically and by means of audio-video communication shall obtain and maintain a surety bond in the amount of $25,000 from a surety or insurance company licensed to do business in this State, and this bond shall be exclusively conditioned on the faithful performance of remote notarial acts or electronic notarial acts by means of audio-video communication. When a notary is required to hold both the $5,000 bond and the $25,000 bond, one bond totaling $30,000 shall satisfy the provisions of this Section.

(c) The bonding company issuing the bond to a notary public or an electronic notary public shall submit verification of the bond information for the notary to the Secretary of State in a format prescribed by the Secretary of State.

History

P.A. 84-322; contingently amended by 2021 P.A. 102-160, § 5, effective January 1, 2022.

5 ILCS 312/2-106 Appointment Recorded by County Clerk. [Repealed]

History

P.A. 84-322; 91-818, § 5; 2017 P.A. 100-201, § 35, effective August 18, 2017; repealed by 2021 P.A. 102-160, § 10, effective July 1, 2022.

ARTICLE III

DUTIES- FEES-AUTHORITY

5 ILCS 312/3-101 Official Seal. [For Effective Date, See Note]

(a) Notary public official seal. Each notary public shall, upon receiving the notary commission from the Secretary of State, obtain an official rubber stamp seal with which the notary shall authenticate his or her official acts. The rubber stamp seal shall contain the following information:

(1) the words "Official Seal";

(2) the notary's official name;

(3) the words "Notary Public", "State of Illinois", and "My commission expires .... (commission expiration date)"; and

(4) a serrated or milled edge border in a rectangular form not more than one inch in height by two and one-half inches in length surrounding the information.

(b) (Blank).

(b-5) Electronic notary public electronic seal and electronic signature. An electronic notarial act must be evidenced by the following, which must be attached to or logically associated with the electronic document that is the subject of the electronic notarial act and which must be immediately perceptible and reproducible:

(1) the electronic signature of the electronic notary public;

(2) the electronic seal of the electronic notary public, which shall look identical to a traditional notary public seal;

(3) the words "Notary Public", "State of Illinois", and "My commission expires (commission expiration date)"; and

(4) language explicitly stating that the electronic notarial act was performed using audiovideo communication, if applicable.

(c) Registered devices. An electronic notary shall register his or her chosen device with the Secretary of State before first use. Thereafter, electronic notary public shall take reasonable steps to ensure that any registered device used to create an electronic seal or electronic signature is current and has not been revoked or terminated by the device's issuing or registering authority.

Upon learning that the technology or device used to create his or her electronic signature has been rendered ineffective or unsecure, an electronic notary public shall cease performing electronic notarial acts until:

(1) a new technology or device is acquired; and

(2) the electronic notary public sends an electronic message to the Secretary of State that includes the electronic signature of the electronic notary public required under paragraph (6) of subsection (b) of Section 2-102 [5 ILCS 312/2-102] relating to the new technology or device.

(d) Electronic signature and seal security.

(1) An electronic notary public shall keep the electronic notary public's electronic signature and electronic seal secure and under the notary public's exclusive control. The electronic notary public shall not allow another person to use his or her electronic signature or electronic seal.

(2) An electronic notary public shall notify an appropriate law enforcement agency, the vendor of the electronic notary technology, and the Secretary of State no later than the next business day after the theft, compromise, or vandalism of the electronic notary public's electronic signature or electronic seal.

(3) The electronic notary public shall not disclose any access information used to affix the electronic notary public's signature and seal except when requested by law enforcement.

(e) Certificate of electronic notarial act. An electronic notary public shall attach his or her electronic signature and electronic seal with the electronic notarial certificate of an electronic document in a manner that is capable of independent verification and renders any subsequent change or modification to the electronic document evident.

(f) The Secretary of State shall have the authority to adopt administrative rules to implement this Section.

History

P.A. 84-322; 95-988, § 5; contingently amended by 2017 P.A. 100-81, § 5, effective January 1, 2018; contingently amended by 2021 P.A. 102-160, § 5, effective January 1, 2022.

5 ILCS 312/3-101.5 Security of electronic signature and seal.

The following requirements apply only to electronic notaries public.

(a) The electronic signature and electronic seal of an electronic notary public must be used only for the purposes of performing electronic notarial acts.

(b) The electronic notary public's electronic signature and electronic seal are deemed to be reliable if the following requirements are met:

(1) it is unique to the electronic notary public;

(2) it is capable of independent verification;

(3) it is retained under the electronic notary public's sole control;

(4) it is attached to or logically associated with the electronic document in a tamper evident manner. Evidence of tampering pursuant to this standard may be used to determine whether the electronic notarial act is valid or invalid;

(5) the electronic notary public has chosen technology or a vendor that meets the minimum requirements established by the Secretary of State and is approved by the Secretary of State; and

(6) the technology adheres to any other standards or requirements set by the Secretary of State in administrative rule.

(c) The electronic notary public shall be prohibited from selling or transferring personal information learned through the course of an electronic notarization, except when required by law, law enforcement, the Secretary of State or court order.

(d) The Secretary of State shall have the authority to adopt administrative rules to implement this Section.

History

Contingently enacted by 2021 P.A. 102-160, § 5.

5 ILCS 312/3-102 Notarial Record; Residential Real Property Transactions.

(a) This Section shall apply to every notarial act in Illinois involving a document of conveyance that transfers or purports to transfer title to residential real property located in Cook County.

(b) As used in this Section, the following terms shall have the meanings ascribed to them:

(1) "Document of Conveyance" shall mean a written instrument that transfers or purports to transfer title effecting a change in ownership to Residential Real Property, excluding:

(i) court-ordered and court-authorized conveyances of Residential Real Property, including without limitation, quit-claim deeds executed pursuant to a marital settlement agreement incorporated into a judgment of dissolution of marriage, and transfers in the administration of a probate estate;

(ii) judicial sale deeds relating to Residential Real Property, including without limitation, sale deeds issued pursuant to proceedings to foreclose a mortgage or execute on a levy to enforce a judgment;

(iii) deeds transferring ownership of Residential Real Property to a trust where the beneficiary is also the grantor;

(iv) deeds from grantors to themselves that are intended to change the nature or type of tenancy by which they own Residential Real Property;

(v) deeds from a grantor to the grantor and another natural person that are intended to establish a tenancy by which the grantor and the other natural person own Residential Real Property;

(vi) deeds executed to the mortgagee in lieu of foreclosure of a mortgage; and

(vii) deeds transferring ownership to a revocable or irrevocable grantor trust where the beneficiary includes the grantor.

(2) "Financial Institution" shall mean a State or federally chartered bank, savings and loan association, savings bank, credit union, or trust company.

(3) "Notarial Record" shall mean the written document created in conformity with this

Section by a notary in connection with Documents of Conveyance.

(4) "Residential Real Property" shall mean a building or buildings located in Cook County, Illinois and containing one to 4 dwelling units or an individual residential condominium unit.

(5) "Title Insurance Agent" shall have the meaning ascribed to it under the Title Insurance Act [215 ILCS 155/1 et seq.].

(6) "Title Insurance Company" shall have the meaning ascribed to it under the Title Insurance Act.

(c) A notary appointed and commissioned as a notary in Illinois shall, in addition to compliance with other provisions of this Act, create a Notarial Record of each notarial act performed in connection with a Document of Conveyance. The Notarial Record shall contain:

(1) The date of the notarial act;

(2) The type, title, or a description of the Document of Conveyance being notarized, and the property index number ("PIN") used to identify the Residential Real Property for assessment or taxation purposes and the common street address for the Residential Real Property that is the subject of the Document of Conveyance;

(3) The signature, printed name, and residence street address of each person whose signature is the subject of the notarial act and a certification by the person that the property is Residential Real Property as defined in this Section, which states "The undersigned grantor hereby certifies that the real property identified in this Notarial Record is Residential Real Property as defined in the Illinois Notary Public Act [5 ILCS 312/1-101 et seq.]".

(4) A description of the satisfactory evidence reviewed by the notary to determine the identity of the person whose signature is the subject of the notarial act;

(5) The date of notarization, the fee charged for the notarial act, the Notary's home or business phone number, the Notary's residence street address, the Notary's commission expiration date, the correct legal name of the Notary's employer or principal, and the business street address of the Notary's employer or principal; and

(6) The notary public shall require the person signing the Document of Conveyance (including an agent acting on behalf of a principal under a duly executed power of attorney), whose signature is the subject of the notarial act, to place his or her right thumbprint on the Notarial Record. If the right thumbprint is not available, then the notary shall have the party use his or her left thumb, or any available finger, and shall so indicate on the Notarial Record. If the party signing the document is physically unable to provide a thumbprint or fingerprint, the notary shall so indicate on the Notarial Record and shall also provide an explanation of that physical condition. The notary may obtain the thumbprint by any means that reliably captures the image of the finger in a physical or electronic medium.

(d) If a notarial act under this Section is performed by a notary who is a principal, employee, or agent of a Title Insurance Company, Title Insurance Agent, Financial Institution, or attorney at law, the notary shall deliver the original Notarial Record to the notary's employer or principal within 14 days after the performance of the notarial act for retention for a period of 7 years as part of the employer's or principal's business records. In the event of a sale or merger of any of the foregoing entities or persons, the successor or assignee of the entity or person shall assume the responsibility to maintain the Notarial Record for the balance of the 7-year business records retention period. Liquidation or other cessation of activities in the ordinary course of business by any of the foregoing entities or persons shall relieve the entity or person from the obligation to maintain Notarial Records after delivery of Notarial Records to the Recorder of Deeds of Cook County, Illinois.

(e) If a notarial act is performed by a notary who is not a principal, employee, or agent of a Title Insurance Company, Title Insurance Agent, Financial Institution, or attorney at law, the notary shall deliver the original Notarial Record within 14 days after the performance of the notarial act to the Recorder of Deeds of Cook County, Illinois for retention for a period of 7 years, accompanied by a filing fee of $5.

(f) The Notarial Record required under subsection (c) of this Section shall be created and maintained for each person whose signature is the subject of a notarial act regarding a Document of Conveyance and shall be in substantially the following form:

NOTARIAL RECORD — RESIDENTIAL REAL PROPERTY TRANSACTIONS

Date Notarized:
Fee: $

The undersigned grantor hereby certifies that the real property identified in this Notarial Record is Residential Real Property as defined in the Illinois Notary Public Act.

Grantor's (Signer's) Printed Name:
Grantor's (Signer's) Signature:
Grantor's (Signer's) Residential Street Address, City, State, and Zip:
Type or Name of Document of Conveyance:
PIN No. of Residential Real Property:
Common Street Address of Residential Real Property:
Thumbprint or Fingerprint:
Description of Means of Identification:
Additional Comments:
Name of Notary Printed:
Notary Phone Number:
Commission Expiration Date:
Residential Street Address of Notary, City, State, and Zip:
Name of Notary's Employer or Principal:
Business Street Address of Notary's Employer or Principal, City, State, and Zip:

(g) No copies of the original Notarial Record may be made or retained by the Notary. The Notary's employer or principal may retain copies of the Notarial Records as part of its business records, subject to applicable privacy and confidentiality standards.

(h) The failure of a notary to comply with the procedure set forth in this Section shall not affect the validity of the Residential Real Property transaction in connection to which the Document of Conveyance is executed, in the absence of fraud.

(i) The Notarial Record or other medium containing the thumbprint or fingerprint required by subsection (c)(6) shall be made available or disclosed only upon receipt of a subpoena duly authorized by a court of competent jurisdiction. Such Notarial Record or other medium shall not be subject to disclosure under the Freedom of Information Act [5 ILCS 140/1 et seq.] and shall not be made available to any other party, other than a party in succession of interest to the party maintaining the Notarial Record or other medium pursuant to subsection (d) or (e).

(j) In the event there is a breach in the security of a Notarial Record maintained pursuant to subsections (d) and (e) by the Recorder of Deeds of Cook County, Illinois, the Recorder shall notify the person identified as the "signer" in the Notarial Record at the signer's residential street address set forth in the Notarial Record. "Breach" shall mean unauthorized acquisition of the fingerprint data contained in the Notarial Record that compromises the security, confidentiality, or integrity of the fingerprint data maintained by the Recorder. The notification shall be in writing and made in the most expedient time possible and without unreasonable delay, consistent with any measures necessary to determine the scope of the breach and restore the reasonable security, confidentiality, and integrity of the Recorder's data system.

(k) Subsections (a) through (i) shall not apply on and after July 1, 2018.

History

P.A. 84-322; 95-988, § 5; 97-508, § 5; 98-29, § 5.

5 ILCS 312/3-103 Notice.

(a) Every notary public who is not an attorney or an accredited immigration representative who advertises the services of a notary public in a language other than English, whether by radio, television, signs, pamphlets, newspapers, electronic communications, or other written communication, with the exception of a single desk plaque, shall include in the document, advertisement, stationery, letterhead, business card, or other comparable written or electronic material the following: notice in English and the language in which the written or electronic communication appears. This notice shall be of a conspicuous size, if in writing or electronic communication, and shall state:

> "I AM NOT AN ATTORNEY LICENSED TO PRACTICE LAW IN ILLINOIS. I AM NOT ALLOWED TO DRAFT LEGAL DOCUMENTS OR RECORDS, NOR MAY I GIVE LEGAL ADVICE ON ANY MATTER, INCLUDING, BUT NOT LIMITED TO, MATTERS OF IMMIGRATION, OR ACCEPT OR CHARGE FEES FOR THE PERFORMANCE OF THOSE ACTIVITIES ".

If such advertisement is by radio or television, the statement may be modified but must include substantially the same message. A notary public shall not, in any document, advertisement, stationery, letterhead, business card, electronic communication, or other comparable written material describing the role of the notary public, literally translate from English into another language terms or titles including, but not limited to, notary public, notary, licensed, attorney, lawyer, or any other term that implies the person is an attorney. To illustrate, the word "notario" is prohibited under this provision. Failure to follow the procedures in this Section shall result in a fine of $1,500 for each written violation. The second violation shall result in permanent revocation of the commission of notary public. Violations shall not preempt or preclude additional appropriate civil or criminal penalties.

(b) All notaries public required to comply with the provisions of subsection (a) shall prominently post at their place of business as recorded with the Secretary of State pursuant to Section 2-102 of this Act [5 ILCS 312/2-102] a schedule of fees established by law which a notary public may charge. The fee schedule shall be written in English and in the non-English language in which notary services were solicited and shall contain the disavowal of legal representation required above in subsection (a), unless such notice of disavowal is already prominently posted.

(c) No notary public, agency or any other person who is not an attorney shall represent, hold themselves out or advertise that they are experts on immigration matters or provide any other assistance that requires legal analysis, legal judgment, or interpretation of the law unless they are a designated entity as defined pursuant to Section 245a.1 of Part 245a of the Code of Federal Regulations (8 CFR 245a.1) or an entity accredited by the Board of Immigration Appeals.

(c-5) In addition to the notice required under subsection (a), every notary public who is subject to subsection (a) shall, prior to rendering notary services or electronic notary services, provide any person seeking notary or electronic notary services services with a written acknowledgment that substantially states, in English and the language used in the advertisement for notary services the following:

> "I AM NOT AN ATTORNEY LICENSED TO PRACTICE LAW IN ILLINOIS. I AM NOT ALLOWED TO DRAFT LEGAL DOCUMENTS OR RECORDS, NOR MAY I GIVE LEGAL ADVICE ON ANY MATTER OR ACCEPT OR CHARGE FEES FOR THE PERFORMANCE OF THOSE ACTIVITIES".

The Office of the Secretary of State shall translate this acknowledgement into Spanish and any other language the Secretary of State may deem necessary to achieve the requirements of this subsection (c-5), and shall make the translations available on the website of the Secretary of State. This acknowledgment shall be signed by the recipient of notary services or electronic notary services before notary services or electronic notary services are rendered, and the notary shall retain copies of all signed acknowledgments throughout their present commission and for 2 years thereafter. Notaries shall provide recipients of notary services or electronic notary services with a copy of their signed acknowledgment at the time services are rendered. This provision shall not apply to notary services or electronic notary services related to documents prepared or produced in accordance with the Illinois Election Code.

(d) Any person who aids, abets or otherwise induces another person to give false information concerning immigration status shall be guilty of a Class A misdemeanor for a first offense and a Class 3 felony for a second or subsequent offense committed within 5 years of a previous conviction for the same offense. Any notary public who violates the provisions of this Section shall be guilty of official misconduct and subject to fine or imprisonment. Nothing in this Section shall preclude any consumer of notary public services from pursuing other civil remedies available under the law.

(e) No notary public who is not an attorney or an accredited representative shall accept payment in exchange for providing legal advice or any other assistance that requires legal analysis, legal judgment, or interpretation of the law.

(f) Violation of subsection (e) is a business offense punishable by a fine of 3 times the amount received for services, or $1,001 minimum, and restitution of the amount paid to the consumer. Nothing in this Section shall be construed to preempt nor preclude additional appropriate civil remedies or criminal charges available under law.

(g) If a notary public or electronic notary public of this State is convicted of a business offense involving a violation of this Act, the Secretary shall automatically revoke the notary public commission or electronic notary public commission of that person on the date that the person's most recent business offense conviction is entered as a final judgment.

History

P.A. 85-593; 93-1001, § 5; contingently amended by 2017 P.A. 100-81, § 5, effective January 1, 2018; contingently amended by 2019 P.A. 101-465, § 5, effective January 1, 2020; contingently amended by 2021 P.A. 102-160, § 5, effective January 1, 2022.

5 ILCS 312/3-104 Maximum Fee.

(a) Except as otherwise provided in this subsection (a), the maximum fee for non-electronic notarization in this State is $5 for any notarial act performed and up to $25 for any notarial act performed pursuant to Section 3-102 [5 ILCS 312/3-102]. Fees for a notary public, agency, or any other person who is not an attorney or an accredited representative filling out immigration forms shall be limited to the following:

(1) $10 per form completion;

(2) $10 per page for the translation of a non-English language into English where such translation is required for immigration forms;

(3) $5 for notarizing;

(4) $3 to execute any procedures necessary to obtain a document required to complete immigration forms; and

(5) A maximum of $75 for one complete application.

Fees authorized under this subsection shall not include application fees required to be submitted with immigration applications.

(b) The maximum fee in this State up to $25 for any electronic notarial act performed pursuant to this Act. An electronic notary public may charge a reasonable fee to recover any cost of providing a copy of an entry or a recording of an audio-video communication in an electronic journal maintained pursuant to Section 3-107 [5 ILCS 312/3-107].

(c) Any person who violates the provisions of subsection (a) or (b) shall be guilty of a Class A misdemeanor for a first offense and a Class 3 felony for a second or subsequent offense committed within 5 years of a previous conviction for the same offense.

(d) Upon his own information or upon complaint of any person, the Attorney General or any State's Attorney, or their designee, may maintain an action for injunctive relief in the court against any notary public or any other person who violates the provisions of subsection (a) or (b) of this Section. These remedies are in addition to, and not in substitution for, other available remedies. If the Attorney General or any State's Attorney fails to bring an action as provided pursuant to this subsection within 90 days of receipt of a complaint, any person may file a civil action to enforce the provisions of this subsection and maintain an action for injunctive relief.

(e) All notaries public must provide itemized receipts and keep records for fees accepted for services provided. Notarial fees must appear on the itemized receipt as separate and distinct from any other charges assessed. Failure to provide itemized receipts and keep records that can be presented as evidence of no wrongdoing shall be construed as a presumptive admission of allegations raised in complaints against the notary for violations related to accepting prohibited fees.

History

P.A. 85-593; 93-1001, § 5; 95-988, § 5; 98-29, § 5; contingently amended by 2021 P.A. 102-160, § 5, effective January 1, 2022.

5 ILCS 312/3-105 Authority.

(a) A notary public shall have authority to perform notarial acts, or electronic notarial acts, if the notary holds an electronic notary public commission, throughout the State so long as the notary resides in the same county in which the notary was commissioned or, if the notary is a resident of a state bordering Illinois, so long as the notary's principal place of work or principal place of business is in the same county in Illinois in which the notary was commissioned.

(b) Except as provided under subsection (c), an electronic notary public who is physically located in this State may perform an electronic notarial act using communication technology in accordance with this Article and any rules adopted by the Secretary of State for a remotely located individual who is physically located: (i) in this State; or (ii) outside of this State, but not outside the United States.

(c) Notwithstanding subsection (b), an electronic notary public may perform an electronic notarial act for a remotely located individual outside of the United States if the record is to be filed with or relates to a matter before a public official or court, governmental entity, or other entity subject to the jurisdiction of the United States or involves property located in the territorial jurisdiction of the United States or involves a transaction substantially connected with the United States.

History

P.A. 84-322; 91-818, § 5; contingently amended by 2021 P.A. 102-160, § 5, effective January 1, 2022.

5 ILCS 312/3-106 Certificate of Authority.

Upon the receipt of a written request, the notarized document, and a fee of $2 payable to the Secretary of State or County Clerk, the Office of the Secretary of State shall provide a certificate of authority in substantially the following form:

> I (Secretary of State) of the State of Illinois, which office is an office of record having a seal, certify that (notary's name), by whom the foregoing or annexed document was notarized or electronically notarized, was, on (insert date), appointed and commissioned a notary public in and for the State of Illinois and that as such, full faith and credit is and ought to be given to this notary's official attestations. In testimony whereof, I have affixed my signature and the seal of this office on (insert date).
>
> (Secretary of State).

History

P.A. 84-322; 91-357, § 8; contingently amended by 2021 P.A. 102-160, § 5, effective January 1, 2022.

5 ILCS 312/6-101 Definitions

(a) "Notarial act" means any act that a notary public of this State is authorized to perform and includes taking an acknowledgment, administering an oath or affirmation, taking a verification upon oath or affirmation, and witnessing or attesting a signature.

(b) "Acknowledgment" means a declaration by a person that the person has executed an instrument for the purposes stated therein and, if the instrument is executed in a representative capacity, that the person signed the instrument with proper authority and executed it as the act of the person or entity represented and identified therein.

(c) "Verification upon oath or affirmation" means a declaration that a statement is true made by a person upon oath or affirmation.

(d) "In a representative capacity" means:

(1) for and on behalf of a corporation, partnership, trust, or other entity, as an authorized officer, agent, partner, trustee, or other representative;

(2) as a public officer, personal representative, guardian, or other representative, in the capacity recited in the instrument;

(3) as an attorney in fact for a principal; or

(4) in any other capacity as an authorized representative of another.

History

P.A. 84-322.

5 ILCS 312/3-107 Journal.

(a) A notary public or an electronic notary public shall keep a journal of each notarial act or electronic notarial act which includes, without limitation, the requirements set by the Secretary of State in administrative rule, but shall not include any electronic signatures of the person for whom an electronic notarial act was performed or any witnesses.

(b) The Secretary of State shall adopt administrative rules that set forth, at a minimum:

(1) the information to be recorded for each notarization or electronic notarization;

(2) the period during which the notary public or electronic notary public must maintain the journal; and

(3) the minimum security requirements for protecting the information in the journal and access to the contents of the journal.

(c) A notary or electronic notary may maintain his or her journal in either paper form or electronic form and may maintain more than one journal or electronic journal to record notarial acts or electronic notarial acts.

(d) The fact that the employer or contractor of a notary or electronic notary public keeps a record of notarial acts or electronic notarial acts does not relieve the notary public of the duties required by this Section. A notary public or electronic notary public shall not surrender the journal to an employer upon termination of employment and an employer shall not retain the journal of an employee when the employment of the notary public or electronic notary public ceases.

(e) If the journal of a notary public or electronic notary public is lost, stolen, or compromised, the notary or electronic notary shall notify the Secretary of State within 10 business days after the discovery of the loss, theft, or breach of security.

(f) Notwithstanding any other provision of this Section or any rules adopted under this Section, neither a notary public nor an electronic notary public is required to keep a journal of or to otherwise record in a journal a notarial act or an electronic notarial act if that act is performed on any of the following documents to be filed by or on behalf of a candidate for public office:

(1) nominating petitions;

(2) petitions of candidacy;

(3) petitions for nomination;

(4) nominating papers; or

(5) nomination papers.

The exemption under this subsection (f) applies regardless of whether the notarial act or electronic notarial act is performed on the documents described in paragraphs (1) through (5) of this subsection before, on, or after the effective date of this amendatory Act of the 103rd General Assembly, and the failure of a notary public or an electronic notary public to keep a journal of or to otherwise record such an act does not affect the validity of the notarial act on that document and is not a violation of this Act. As used in this subsection (f), "public office" has the meaning given in Section 9-1.10 of the Election Code.

History

Contingently enacted by 2021 P.A. 102-160, § 5, effective January 1, 2022.

ARTICLE IV

CHANGE OF NAME OR MOVE FROM COUNTY

5 ILCS 312/4-101 Changes causing commission to cease to be in effect.

(a) When any notary public legally changes his or her name, changes his or her residential address or business address, or email address, without notifying the Index Department of the Secretary of State in writing within 30 days thereof, or, if the notary public is a resident of a state bordering Illinois, no longer maintains a principal place of work or principal place of business in the same county in Illinois in which he or she was commissioned, the commission of that notary ceases to be in effect. When the commission of a notary public ceases to be in effect, his or her notarial seal or electronic notary seal shall be surrendered to the Secretary of State, and his or her certificate of notarial commission or certificate of electronic notarial commission shall be destroyed. These individuals who desire to again become a notary public must file a new application, bond, and oath with the Secretary of State.

(b) Any change to the information submitted by an electronic notary public in registering to perform electronic notarial acts in compliance with any Section of this Act shall be reported by the notary within 30 business days to the Secretary of State.

(c) Any notary public or electronic notary public that fails to comply with this Section shall be prohibited from obtaining a new commission for a period of not less than 5 years.

History

P.A. 85-1209; 91-818, § 5; contingently amended by 2018 P.A. 100-809, § 5, effective January 1, 2019; contingently amended by 2021 P.A. 102-160, § 5, effective January 1, 2022.

ARTICLE V

REAPPOINTMENT AS A NOTARY PUBLIC

5 ILCS 312/5-101 Reappointment.

No person is automatically reappointed as a notary public or electronic notary public. At least 60 days prior to the expiration of a commission, the Secretary of State shall mail notice of the expiration date to the holder of a commission. Every notary public or electronic notary public who is an applicant for reappointment shall comply with the provisions of Article II of this Act [5 ILCS 312/2-101 et seq.].

History

P.A. 84-322; contingently amended by 2021 P.A. 102-160, § 5, effective January 1, 2022.

ARTICLE VI

NOTARIAL ACTS AND FORMS

5 ILCS 312/6-101 Definitions

(a) "Notarial act" means any act that a notary public of this State is authorized to perform and includes taking an acknowledgment, administering an oath or affirmation, taking a verification upon oath or affirmation, and witnessing or attesting a signature.

(b) "Acknowledgment" means a declaration by a person that the person has executed an instrument for the purposes stated therein and, if the instrument is executed in a representative capacity, that the person signed the instrument with proper authority and executed it as the act of the person or entity represented and identified therein.

(c) "Verification upon oath or affirmation" means a declaration that a statement is true made by a person upon oath or affirmation.

(d) "In a representative capacity" means:

(1) for and on behalf of a corporation, partnership, trust, or other entity, as an authorized officer, agent, partner, trustee, or other representative;

(2) as a public officer, personal representative, guardian, or other representative, in the capacity recited in the instrument;

(3) as an attorney in fact for a principal; or

(4) in any other capacity as an authorized representative of another.

History

P.A. 84-322.

5 ILCS 312/6-102 Notarial Acts.

(a) In taking an acknowledgment, the notary public must determine, either from personal knowledge or from satisfactory evidence, that the person appearing before the notary and making the acknowledgment is the person whose true signature is on the instrument.

(b) In taking a verification upon oath or affirmation, the notary public must determine, either from personal knowledge or from satisfactory evidence, that the person appearing before the notary and making the verification is the person whose true signature is on the statement verified.

(c) In witnessing or attesting a signature, the notary public must determine, either from personal knowledge or from satisfactory evidence, that the signature is that of the person appearing before the notary and named therein.

(d) A notary public has satisfactory evidence that a person is the person whose true signature is on a document if that person:

(1) is personally known to the notary;

(2) is identified upon the oath or affirmation of a credible witness personally known to the notary; or

(3) is identified on the basis of identification documents. Identification documents are documents that are valid at the time of the notarial act, issued by a state agency, federal government agency, or consulate, and bearing the photographic image of the individual's face and signature of the individual.

(e) A notary public or electronic notary public shall have no obligation to perform any notarial or electronic notarial act, and may refuse to perform a notarial or electronic notarial act without further explanation.

History

P.A. 84-322; 95-988, § 5; 97-397, § 5; 98-29, § 5; contingently amended by 2021 P.A. 102-160, § 5, effective January 1, 2022.

5 ILCS 312/6-102.5 Remote notarial acts.

(a) Any commissioned notary public may perform any notarial act described under Section 6-102 [5 ILCS 312/6-102] remotely, after first determining, either from personal knowledge or from satisfactory evidence, that the signature is that of the person appearing before the notary and named therein. A notary public has satisfactory evidence that a person is the person whose true signature is on a document if that person:

(1) is personally known to the notary;

(2) is identified upon the oath or affirmation of a credible witness personally known to the notary; or

(3) is identified on the basis of identification documents. Identification documents are documents that are (i) valid at the time of the notarial act, (ii) issued by a State agency, federal government agency, or consulate, and (iii) bearing the photographic image of the individual's face and signature of the individual.

(b) A remote notarial action must be performed in accordance with the following audio-video communication requirements:

(1) Two-way audio-video communication technology must allow for remotely located notaries and principals to engage in direct, contemporaneous interaction between the individual signing the document (signatory) and the witness by sight and sound.

(2) The two-way audio video communication technology must be recorded and preserved by the signatory or the signatory's designee for a period of at least 3 years.

(3) The signatory must attest to being physically located in Illinois during the two-way audiovideo communication.

(4) The signatory must affirmatively state on the two-way audio-video communication what document the signatory is signing.

(5) Each page of the document being witnessed must be shown to the witness on the two-way audio-video communication technology in a means clearly legible to the witness.

(6) The act of signing must be captured sufficiently up close on the two-way audio-video communication for the witness to observe.

(c) Application of the notary's seal and signature:

(1) The signatory must transmit by overnight mail, fax, or electronic means a legible copy of the entire signed document directly to the notary no later than the day after the document is signed.

(2) The notary must sign the transmitted copy of the document as a witness and transmit the signed copy of the document back to the signatory via overnight mail, fax, or electronic means within 24 hours after receipt.

(3) If necessary, the notary may sign the original signed document as of the date of the original execution by the signatory provided that the witness receives the original signed document together with the electronically witnessed copy within 30 days after the date of the remote notarization.

(d) The Secretary of State shall adopt administrative rules to implement this Section.

History

Contingently enacted by 2021 P.A. 102-160, § 5, effective January 1, 2022.

5 ILCS 312/6-103 Certificate of Notarial Acts.

(a) A notarial act must be evidenced by a certificate signed and dated by the notary public.

The certificate must include identification of the jurisdiction in which the notarial act is performed and the official seal of office.

(b) A certificate of a notarial act is sufficient if it meets the requirements of subsection (a) and it:

(1) is in the short form set forth in Section 6-105 [5 ILCS 312/6-105];

(2) is in a form otherwise prescribed by the law of this State; or

(3) sets forth the actions of the notary public and those are sufficient to meet the requirements of the designated notarial act.

(c) At the time of a notarial act, a notary public shall officially sign every notary certificate and affix the rubber stamp seal clearly and legibly using black ink, so that it is capable of photographic reproduction. The illegibility of any of the information required under this Section does not affect the validity of a transaction.

History

P.A. 84-322; 2017 P.A. 100-81, § 5, effective January 1, 2018.

5 ILCS 312/6-104 Acts prohibited.

(a) A notary public shall not use any name or initial in signing certificates other than that by which the notary was commissioned.

(b) A notary public shall not acknowledge any instrument in which the notary's name appears as a party to the transaction.

(c) A notary public shall not affix his signature to a blank form of affidavit or certificate of acknowledgment.

(d) A notary public shall not take the acknowledgment of or administer an oath to any person whom the notary actually knows to have been adjudged mentally ill by a court of competent jurisdiction and who has not been restored to mental health as a matter of record.

(e) A notary public shall not take the acknowledgment of any person who is blind until the notary has read the instrument to such person.

(f) A notary public shall not take the acknowledgment of any person who does not speak or understand the English language, unless the nature and effect of the instrument to be notarized is translated into a language which the person does understand.

(g) A notary public shall not change anything in a written instrument after it has been signed by anyone.

(h) No notary public shall be authorized to prepare any legal instrument, or fill in the blanks of an instrument, other than a notary certificate; however, this prohibition shall not prohibit an attorney, who is also a notary public, from performing notarial acts for any document prepared by that attorney.

(i) If a notary public accepts or receives any money from any one to whom an oath has been administered or on behalf of whom an acknowledgment has been taken for the purpose of transmitting or forwarding such money to another and willfully fails to transmit or forward such money promptly, the notary is personally liable for any loss sustained because of such failure. The person or persons damaged by such failure may bring an action to recover damages, together with interest and reasonable attorney fees, against such notary public or his bondsmen.

(j) A notary public shall not perform any notarial act when his or her commission is

suspended or revoked, nor shall he or she fail to comply with any term of suspension which may be imposed for violation of this Section.

(k) No notary public shall be authorized to explain, certify, or verify the contents of any document; however, this prohibition shall not prohibit an attorney, who is also a notary public, from performing notarial acts for any document prepared by that attorney.

(l) A notary public shall not represent himself or herself as an electronic notary public if the person has not been commissioned as an electronic notary public by the Secretary of State.

(m) No person shall knowingly create, manufacture, or distribute software or hardware for the purpose of allowing a person to act as an electronic notary public without being commissioned in accordance with this Act. A violation of this subsection (m) is a Class A misdemeanor.

(n) No person shall wrongfully obtain, conceal, damage, or destroy the technology or device used to create the electronic signature or seal of an electronic notary public. A violation of this subsection (n) is a Class A misdemeanor.

(o) A notary public shall not sell, rent, transfer, or otherwise make available to a third party, other than the electronic notarization platform, the contents of the notarial journal, audio-video recordings, or any other record associated with any notarial act, including personally identifiable information, except when required by law, law enforcement, the Secretary of State, or a court order. Upon written request of a third party, which request must include the name of the parties, the type of document, and the month and year in which a record was notarized, a notary public may supply a copy of the line item representing the requested transaction after personally identifying information has been redacted.

(p) The Secretary of State may suspend the commission of a notary or electronic notary who fails to produce any journal entry within 10 days after receipt of a request from the Secretary of State.

(q) Upon surrender, revocation, or expiration of a commission as a notary or electronic notary, all notarial records or electronic notarial records required under this Section, except as otherwise provided by law, must be kept by the notary public or electronic notary for a period of 5 years after the termination of the registration of the notary public or electronic notary public.

History

P.A. 85-421; contingently amended by 2017 P.A. 100-81, § 5, effective January 1, 2018; contingently amended by 2018 P.A. 100-809, § 5, effective January 1, 2019; contingently amended by 2021 P.A. 102-160, § 5, effective January 1, 2022.

5 ILCS 312/6-105 Short Forms

The following short form certificates of notarial acts are sufficient for the purposes indicated.

(a) For an acknowledgment in an individual capacity:

State of _____
County of _____

This instrument was acknowledged before me on _____
(date) by _____ (name/s of person/s).

_____ (Signature of Notary Public)
(Seal)

(b) For an acknowledgment in a representative capacity:

State of _____
County of _____

This instrument was acknowledged before me on _____
(date) by _____ (name/s of person/s) as _____
_____ (type of authority, e.g., officer, trustee,
etc.) of _____ (name of party on behalf of whom instrument was executed).

_____ (Signature of Notary Public)
(Seal)

(c) For a verification upon oath or affirmation:

State of _____
County of _____

Signed and sworn (or affirmed) to before me on _____
(date) by _____ (name/s of person/s making statement).

_____ (Signature of Notary Public)

(Seal)

(d) For witnessing or attesting a signature:

State of _____

County of _____

Signed or attested before me on _____ (date) by
_____ (name/s of person/s).

_____ (Signature of Notary Public)

(Seal)

History

P.A. 84-322.

ARTICLE VI-A.

ELECTRONIC NOTARIAL ACTS AND FORMS

5 ILCS 312/6A-101 Requirements for systems and providers of electronic notarial technology.

(a) An electronic notarization system shall comply with this Act and any rules adopted by the Secretary of State.

(b) An electronic notarization system requiring enrollment shall enroll only persons commissioned as electronic notaries public by the Secretary of State.

(c) An electronic notarization vendor shall take reasonable steps to ensure that an electronic notary public who has enrolled to use the system has the knowledge to use it to perform electronic notarial acts in compliance with this Act.

(d) A provider of an electronic notarization system requiring enrollment shall notify the Secretary of State of the name of each electronic notary public who enrolls in the system within 5 days after enrollment by means prescribed by rule by the Secretary of State.

(e) The Secretary of State shall adopt administrative rules that set forth the requirements a provider of electronic notarization technology must meet in order to be approved for use in the State of Illinois. At a minimum, those administrative rules shall establish:

(1) minimum standards ensuring a secure means of authentication to be employed to protect the integrity of the electronic notary's electronic seal and electronic signature;

(2) minimum standards ensuring that documents electronically notarized be tamper-evident and protected from unauthorized use; and

(3) requirements for competent operation of the electronic platform.

History

Contingently enacted by 2021 P.A. 102-160, § 5, effective January 1, 2022.

5 ILCS 312/6A-102 Electronic notary not liable for system failure.

An electronic notary public who exercised reasonable care enrolling in and using an electronic notarization system shall not be liable for any damages resulting from the system's failure to comply with the requirements of this Act. Any provision in a contract or agreement between the electronic notary public and provider that attempts to waive this immunity shall be null, void, and of no effect.

History

Contingently enacted by 2021 P.A. 102-160, § 5, effective January 1, 2022.

5 ILCS 312/6A-103 Electronic notarial acts. [For Effective Date, See Note]

(a) An electronic notary public:

(1) is a notary public for purposes of this Act and is subject to all provisions of this Act;

(2) may perform notarial acts as provided by this Act in addition to performing electronic notarizations; and

(3) may perform an electronic notarization authorized under this Article.

(b) In performing an electronic notarization, an electronic notary public shall verify the identity of a person creating an electronic signature at the time that the signature is taken by using two-way audio and video conference technology that meets the requirements of this Act and rules adopted under this Article. For the purposes of performing an electronic notarial act for a person using audio-video communication, an electronic notary public has satisfactory or documentary evidence of the identity of the person if the electronic notary public confirms the identity of the person by:

(1) the electronic notary public's personal knowledge of the person creating the electronic signature; or

(2) each of the following:

(A) remote electronic presentation by the person creating the electronic signature of a

government-issued identification credential, including a passport or driver's license, that contains the signature and a photograph of the person;

(B) credential analysis of the front and back of the government-issued identification credential and the data thereon; and

(C) a dynamic knowledge-based authentication assessment.

(c) An electronic notary public may perform any of the acts set forth in Section 6-102 [5 ILCS 312/6-102] using audio-video communication in accordance with this Section and any rules adopted by the Secretary of State.

(d) If an electronic notarial act is performed using audio-video communication:

(1) the technology must allow the persons communicating to see and speak to each other simultaneously;

(2) the signal transmission must be in real time; and

(3) the electronic notarial act must be recorded.

(e) The validity of the electronic notarial act will be determined by applying the laws of the State of Illinois.

(f) The electronic notarial certificate for an electronic notarization must include a notation that the notarization is an electronic notarization.

(g) When performing an electronic notarization, an electronic notary public shall complete an electronic notarial certificate and attach or logically associate the electronic notary's electronic signature and seal to that certificate in a tamper evident manner. Evidence of tampering pursuant to this standard may be used to determine whether the electronic notarial act is valid or invalid.

(h) The liability, sanctions, and remedies for improper performance of electronic notarial acts are the same as described and provided by law for the improper performance of non-electronic notarial acts as described under Section 7-108 [5 ILCS 312/7-108].

(i) Electronic notarial acts need to fulfill certain basic requirements to ensure non-repudiation and the capability of being authenticated by the Secretary of State for purposes of issuing apostilles and certificates of authentication. The requirements are as follows:

(1) the fact of the electronic notarial act, including the electronic notary's identity, signature, and electronic commission status, must be verifiable by the Secretary of State; and

(2) the notarized electronic document will be rendered ineligible for authentication by the Secretary of State if it is improperly modified after the time of electronic notarization, including any unauthorized alterations to the document content, the electronic notarial certificate, the electronic notary public's electronic signature, or the electronic notary public's official electronic seal.

History

Contingently enacted by 2021 P.A. 102-160, § 5, effective January 1, 2022.

5 ILCS 312/6A-104 Requirements for audio-video communication.

(a) An electronic notary public shall arrange for a recording to be made of each electronic notarial act performed using audio-video communication. The audio-video recording required by this Section shall be in addition to the journal entry for the electronic notarial act required by Section 3-107 [5 ILCS 312/3-107]. Before performing any electronic notarial act using audiovideo communication, the electronic notary public must inform all participating persons that the electronic notarization will be electronically recorded.

(b) If the person for whom the electronic notarial act is being performed is identified by personal knowledge, the recording of the electronic notarial act must include an explanation by the electronic notary public as to how he or she knows the person and how long he or she has known the person.

(c) If the person for whom the electronic notarial act is being performed is identified by a credible witness:

(1) the credible witness must appear before the electronic notary public; and

(2) the recording of the electronic notarial act must include:

(A) a statement by the electronic notary public as to whether he or she identified the credible witness by personal knowledge or satisfactory evidence; and

(B) an explanation by the credible witness as to how he or she knows the person for whom the electronic notarial act is being performed and how long he or she has known the person.

(d) An electronic notary public shall keep a recording made pursuant to this Section for a period of not less than 7 years, regardless of whether the electronic notarial act was actually completed.

(e) An electronic notary public who performs an electronic notarial act for a principal by means of audio-video communication shall be located within the State of Illinois at the time the electronic notarial act is performed. The electronic notary public shall include a statement in the electronic notarial certificate to indicate that the electronic notarial act was performed by means of audio-video communication. The statement may also be included in the electronic notarial seal.

(f) An electronic notary public who performs an electronic notarial act for a principal by means of audio-video communication shall:

(1) be located within this State at the time the electronic notarial act is performed;

(2) execute the electronic notarial act in a single recorded session that complies with Section 6A-103 [5 ILCS 312/6A-103];

(3) be satisfied that any electronic record that is electronically signed, acknowledged, or otherwise presented for electronic notarization by the principal is the same record electronically signed by the electronic notary;

(4) be satisfied that the quality of the audio-video communication is sufficient to make the determination required for the electronic notarial act under this Act and any other law of this State; and

(5) identify the venue for the electronic notarial act as the jurisdiction within Illinois where the notary is physically located while performing the act.

(g) An electronic notarization system used to perform electronic notarial acts by means of audio-video communication shall conform to the requirements set forth in this Act and by administrative rules adopted by the Secretary of State.

(h) The provisions of Section 3-107 [5 ILCS 312/3-107] related respectively to security, inspection, copying, and disposition of the journal shall also apply to security, inspection, copying, and disposition of audio-video recordings required by this Section.

(i) The Secretary of State shall adopt administrative rules to implement this Section.

History

Contingently enacted by 2021 P.A. 102-160, § 5, effective January 1, 2022.

5 ILCS 312/6A-105 Electronic certificate of notarial acts.

(a) An electronic notarial certificate must be evidenced by an electronic notarial certificate signed and dated by the electronic notary public. The electronic notarial certificate must include identification of the jurisdiction in which the electronic notarial act is performed and the electronic seal of the electronic notary public.

(b) An electronic notarial certificate of an electronic notarial act is sufficient if it meets the requirements of subsection (a) and it:

(1) is in the short form set forth in 6-105 [5 ILCS 312/6-105];

(2) is in a form otherwise prescribed by the law of this State; or

(3) sets forth the actions of the electronic notary public and those are sufficient to meet the requirements of the designated electronic notarial act.

(c) At the time of an electronic notarial act, an electronic notary public shall electronically sign every electronic notarial certificate and electronically affix the electronic seal clearly and legibly, so that it is capable of photographic reproduction. The illegibility of any of the information required under this Section does not affect the validity of a transaction.

History

Contingently enacted by 2021 P.A. 102-160, § 5, effective January 1, 2022.

5 ILCS 312/6A-106 Electronic acknowledgments; physical presence.

(a) For purposes of this Act, a person may appear before the person taking the acknowledgment by:

(1) being in the same physical location as the other person and close enough to see, hear, communicate with, and exchange tangible identification credentials with that person; or

(2) being outside the physical presence of the other person, but interacting with the other person by means of communication technology.

(b) If the acknowledging person is outside the physical presence of the person taking the acknowledgment, the certification of acknowledgment must indicate that the notarial act was performed by means of communication technology. A form of certificate of acknowledgment as provided by the Secretary of State, which may include the use of a remote online notarial certificate, is sufficient for purposes of this subsection (b) if it substantially reads as follows:

> "The foregoing instrument was acknowledged before me by means of communication technology this (date) by ... (each form continued as sufficient for its respective purposes.)".

History

Contingently enacted by 2021 P.A. 102-160, § 5, effective January 1, 2022.

ARTICLE VII

LIABILITY AND REVOCATION

5 ILCS 312/7-101 Liability of Notary and Surety.

A notary public and the surety on the notary's bond are liable to the persons involved for all damages caused by the notary's official misconduct. Upon the filing of any claim against a notary public, the entity that has issued the bond for the notary shall notify the Secretary of State of whether payment was made and the circumstances which led to the claim.

History

P.A. 84-322; 2018 P.A. 100-809, § 5, effective January 1, 2019.

5 ILCS 312/7-102 Liability of Employer of Notary

The employer of a notary public is also liable to the persons involved for all damages caused by the notary's official misconduct, if:

(a) the notary public was acting within the scope of the notary's employment at the time the notary engaged in the official misconduct; and

(b) the employer consented to the notary public's official misconduct.

History

P.A. 84-322.

5 ILCS 312/7-103 Cause of Damages

It is not essential to a recovery of damages that a notary's official misconduct be the only cause of the damages.

History

P.A. 84-322.

5 ILCS 312/7-104 Official Misconduct Defined

Official Misconduct Defined. The term "official misconduct" generally means the wrongful exercise of a power or the wrongful performance of a duty and is fully defined in Section 33-3 of the Criminal Code of 2012 [720 ILCS 5/33-3]. The term "wrongful" as used in the definition of official misconduct means unauthorized, unlawful, abusive, negligent, reckless, or injurious.

History

P.A. 85-293; 97-1150, § 25.

5 ILCS 312/7-105 Official Misconduct

(a) A notary public who knowingly and willfully commits any official misconduct is guilty of a Class A misdemeanor.

(b) A notary public who recklessly or negligently commits any official misconduct is guilty of a Class B misdemeanor.

History

P.A. 84-322.

5 ILCS 312/7-106 Willful Impersonation.

(a) Any person who acts as, or otherwise willfully impersonates, a notary public while not lawfully appointed and commissioned to perform notarial acts is guilty of a Class A misdemeanor.

(b) Any notary public or other person who is not an electronic notary public that impersonates an electronic notary public to perform electronic notarial acts is guilty of a Class A misdemeanor.

History

P.A. 84-322; contingently amended by 2021 P.A. 102-160, § 5, effective January 1, 2022.

5 ILCS 312/7-107 Wrongful Possession.

(a) No person may unlawfully possess, obtain, conceal, damage, or destroy a notary's official seal.

(b) No person may unlawfully possess, conceal, damage, or destroy the certificate, disk, coding, card, program, software, or hardware enabling an electronic notary public to affix an official electronic signature or seal.

(c) Any person who violates this Section shall be guilty of a misdemeanor and punishable upon conviction by a fine not exceeding $1,000.

History

P.A. 84-322; contingently amended by 2021 P.A. 102-160, § 5, effective January 1, 2022.

5 ILCS 312/7-108 Reprimand, suspension, and revocation of commission.

(a) The Secretary of State may revoke the commission of any notary public who, during the current term of appointment:

(1) submits an application for commission and appointment as a notary public which contains substantial and material misstatement or omission of fact;

(2) is convicted of any felony, misdemeanors, including those defined in Part C, Articles 16, 17, 18, 19, and 21, and Part E, Articles 31, 32, and 33 of the Criminal Code of 2012 [720 ILCS 5/16-0.1 et seq., 720 ILCS 5/17-0.5 et seq., 720 ILCS 5/18-1 et seq., 720 ILCS 5/19-1 et seq., 720 ILCS 5/21-1 et seq., and 720 ILCS 5/31-1 et seq., 720 ILCS 5/32-1 et seq., 720 ILCS 5/33-1 et seq.], or official misconduct under this Act; or

(3) is a licensed attorney and has been sanctioned, suspended, or disbarred by the Illinois Attorney Registration and Disciplinary Commission or the Illinois Supreme Court.

(b) Whenever the Secretary of State believes that a violation of this Article has occurred, he or she may investigate any such violation. The Secretary may also investigate possible violations of this Article upon a signed written complaint on a form designated by the Secretary.

(c) A notary's failure to cooperate or respond to an investigation by the Secretary of State is a failure by the notary to fully and faithfully discharge the responsibilities and duties of a notary and shall result in suspension or revocation of the notary's commission or the electronic notary's commission.

(d) All written complaints which on their face appear to establish facts which, if proven true, would constitute an act of misrepresentation or fraud in notarization or electronic notarization, or misrepresentation or fraud on the part of the notary, may be investigated by the Secretary of State to determine whether cause exists to reprimand, suspend, or revoke the commission of the notary.

(e) The Secretary of State may deliver a written official warning and reprimand to a notary, or may revoke or suspend a notary's commission or an electronic notary's commission, for any of the following:

(1) a notary's official misconduct, as defined under Section 7-104 [5 ILCS 312/7-104];

(2) any ground for which an application for appointment as a notary may be denied for failure to complete application requirements as provided under Section 2-102 [5 ILCS 312/2-102];

(3) any prohibited act provided under Section 6-104 [5 ILCS 312/6-104]; or

(4) a violation of any provision of the general statutes.

(f) After investigation and upon a determination by the Secretary of State that one or moreprohibited acts have been performed in the notarization or electronic notarization of a document, the Secretary shall, after considering the extent of the prohibited act and the degree of culpability of the notary, order one or more of the following courses of action:

(1) issue a letter of warning to the notary, including the Secretary's findings;

(2) order suspension of the commission of the notary or electronic commission of the notary for a period of time designated by the Secretary;

(3) order revocation of the commission of the notary or electronic commission of the notary;

(4) refer the allegations to the appropriate State's Attorney's Office or the Attorney General for criminal investigation; or

(5) refer the allegations to the Illinois Attorney Registration and Disciplinary Commission for disciplinary proceedings.

(g) After a notary receives notice from the Secretary of State that his or her commission has been revoked, that notary shall immediately deliver his or her official seal to the Secretary. After an electronic notary public receives notice from the Secretary of State that his or her electronic commission has been revoked, the electronic notary public shall immediately notify the electronic notary's chosen technology provider, and to the extent possible, destroy or remove the software used for electronic notarizations.

(h) A notary whose appointment has been revoked due to a violation of this Act shall not be eligible for a new commission as a notary public in this State for a period of at least 5 years from the date of the final revocation.

(i) A notary may voluntarily resign from appointment by notifying the Secretary of State in writing of his or her intention to do so, and by physically returning his or her stamp to the Secretary. An electronic notary public may voluntarily resign from appointment by notifying the Secretary of State in writing of his or her intention to do so, and by notifying the electronic notary's chosen technology provider, and to the extent possible, destroy or remove the software used for electronic notarizations. A voluntary resignation shall not stop or preclude any investigation into a notary's conduct, or prevent further suspension or revocation by the Secretary, who may pursue any such investigation to a conclusion and issue any finding.

(j) Upon a determination by a sworn law enforcement officer that the allegations raised by the complaint are founded, and the notary has received notice of suspension or revocation from the Secretary of State, the notary is entitled to an administrative hearing.

(k) The Secretary of State shall adopt administrative hearing rules applicable to this Section that are consistent with the Illinois Administrative Procedure Act [5 ILCS 100/1-1 et seq.].

(l) Any revocation, resignation, expiration, or suspension of the commission of a notary public terminates or suspends any commission to notarize electronically.

(m) A notary public may terminate registration to notarize electronically and maintain his or her underlying notary public commission upon directing a written notification of the change to the Secretary of State within 30 days.

History

P.A. 84-322; contingently amended by 2018 P.A. 100-809, § 5, effective January 1, 2019; contingently amended by 2019 P.A. 101-81, § 20, effective July 12, 2019; contingently amended by 2021 P.A. 102-160, § 5, effective January 1, 2022.

5 ILCS 312/7-109 Action for Injunction, Unauthorized Practice of Law

Upon his own information or upon complaint of any person, the Attorney General or any State's Attorney, or their designee, may maintain an action for injunctive relief in the circuit court against any notary public who renders, offers to render, or holds himself or herself out as rendering any service constituting the unauthorized practice of the law. Any organized bar association in this State may intervene in the action, at any stage of the proceeding, for good cause shown. The action may also be maintained by an organized bar association in this State. These remedies are in addition to, and not in substitution for, other available remedies.

History

P.A. 84-322.

5 ILCS 312/7-110 Applicable law; conflict of law.

(a) The validity of any notarization, including an electronic notarization, shall be determined by applying the laws of this State, regardless of the physical location of the principal at the time of a remote notarization.

(b) An electronic notary public authorized to perform electronic notarizations is subject to and must comply with this Act.

(c) If a conflict between a provision of this Section and another law of this State, this Section controls.

History

Contingently enacted by 2021 P.A. 102-160, § 5, effective January 1, 2022.

ARTICLE VIII.

REPEALER AND EFFECTIVE DATE

5 ILCS 312/8-101 [Repealer]

Section 2 of "An Act to increase the fee for issuing commissions to notaries public", approved June 3, 1897, as amended, is repealed.

History

P.A. 84-322.

5 ILCS 312/8-102 [Repealer]

Section 28 of "An Act concerning fees and salaries, and to classify the several counties of this State with reference thereto", approved March 29, 1872, as amended, is repealed.

History

P.A. 84-322.

5 ILCS 312/8-103 [Repealer]

"An Act to provide for the appointment, qualification and duties of notaries public and certifying their official acts and to provide for fines and penalties for the violation thereof", approved April 5, 1872, as amended, is repealed.

History

P.A. 84-322.

5 ILCS 312/8-104 [Effective date]

This Act takes effect July 1, 1986.

History

P.A. 84-322.

CHAPTER 765. PROPERTY

ACT 30. UNIFORM RECOGNITION OF ACKNOWLEDGMENTS ACT

765 ILCS 30/1. Short title.

This Act may be cited as the Uniform Recognition of Acknowledgments Act.

History

P.A. 76-1105.

765 ILCS 30/2. Recognition of notarial acts performed outside this State.

For the purposes of this Act, "notarial acts" means acts which the laws and regulations of this State authorize notaries public of this State to perform, including the administering of oaths and affirmations, taking proof of execution and acknowledgments of instruments, and attesting documents. Notarial acts may be performed outside this State for use in this State with the same effect as if performed by a notary public of this State by the following persons authorized pursuant to the laws and regulations of other governments in addition to any other person authorized by the laws and regulations of this State:

(1) a notary public authorized to perform notarial acts in the place in which the act is performed;

(2) a judge, clerk, or deputy clerk of any court of record in the place in which the notarial act is performed;

(3) an officer of the foreign service of the United States, a consular agent, or any other

person authorized by regulation of the United States Department of State to perform notarial acts in the place in which the act is performed;

(4) a commissioned officer in active service with the Armed Forces of the United States and any other person authorized by regulation of the Armed Forces to perform notarial acts if the notarial act is performed for one of the following or his dependents: a merchant seaman of the United States, a member of the Armed Forces of the United States, or any other person serving with or accompanying the Armed Forces of the United States; or

(5) any other person authorized to perform notarial acts in the place in which the act is performed.

History

P.A. 76-1105.

765 ILCS 30/3. Authentication of authority of officer.

(a) If the notarial act is performed by any of the persons described in paragraphs 1 to 4, inclusive of Section 2, other than a person authorized to perform notarial acts by the laws or regulations of a foreign country, the signature, rank, or title and serial number, if any, of the person are sufficient proof of the authority of a holder of that rank or title to perform the act. Further proof of his authority is not required.

(b) If the notarial act is performed by a person authorized by the laws or regulations of a foreign country to perform the act, there is sufficient proof of the authority of that person to act if:

(1) either a foreign service officer of the United States resident in the country in which the act is performed or a diplomatic or consular officer of the foreign country resident in the United States certifies that a person holding that office is authorized to perform the act;

(2) the official seal of the person performing the notarial act is affixed to the document; or

(3) the title and indication of authority to perform notarial acts of the person appears either in a digest of foreign law or in a list customarily used as a source of such information.

(c) If the notarial act is performed by a person other than one described in subsections (a) and (b), there is sufficient proof of the authority of that person to act if the clerk of a court of record in the place in which the notarial act is performed certifies to the official character of that person and to his authority to perform the notarial act.

(d) The signature and title of the person performing the act are prima facie evidence that he is a person with the designated title and that the signature is genuine.

History

P.A. 76-1105.

765 ILCS 30/4. Certificate of person taking acknowledgment.

The person taking an acknowledgment shall certify that:

(1) the person acknowledging appeared before him and acknowledged he executed the instrument; and

(2) the person acknowledging was known to the person taking the acknowledgment or that the person taking the acknowledgment had satisfactory evidence that the person acknowledging was the person described in and who executed the instrument.

P.A. 76-1105; 91-357, § 267.

765 ILCS 30/5. Recognition of certificate of acknowledgment.

The form of a certificate of acknowledgment used by a person whose authority is recognized under Section 2 shall be accepted in this State if:

(1) the certificate is in a form prescribed by the laws or regulations of this State;

(2) the certificate is in a form prescribed by the laws or regulations applicable in the place in which the acknowledgment is taken; or

(3) the certificate contains the words "acknowledged before me" or their substantial equivalent.

P.A. 76-1105; 91-357, § 267.

765 ILCS 30/6. Certificate of acknowledgment.

The words "acknowledged before me" means

(1) that the person acknowledging appeared before the person taking the acknowledgment in a manner prescribed by the laws or regulations applicable in the place in which the acknowledgment is taken,

(2) that he acknowledged he executed the instrument,

(3) that, in the case of:

(i) a natural person, he executed the instrument for the purposes therein stated;

(ii) a corporation, the officer or agent acknowledged he held the position or title set forth in the instrument and certificate, he signed the instrument on behalf of the corporation by proper authority, and the instrument was the act of the corporation for the purpose therein stated;

(iii) a partnership, the partner or agent acknowledged he signed the instrument on behalf of the partnership by proper authority and he executed the instrument as the act of the partnership for the purposes therein stated;

(iv) a person acknowledging as principal by an attorney in fact, he executed the instrument by proper authority as the act of the principal for the purposes therein stated;

(v) a person acknowledging as a public officer, trustee, administrator, guardian, or other representative, he signed the instrument by proper authority and he executed the instrument in the capacity and for the purposes therein stated; and

(4) that the person taking the acknowledgment either knew or had satisfactory evidence that the person acknowledging was the person named in the instrument or certificate.

P.A. 76-1105; 2021 P.A. 102-500, § 5, effective January 1, 2022.

765 ILCS 30/7. Short forms of acknowledgment.

(a) The forms of acknowledgment set forth in this Section may be used and are sufficient for their respective purposes under any law of this State, whether executed in this State or any other State. The forms shall be known as "Statutory Short Forms of Acknowledgment" and may be referred to by that name. The authorization of the forms in this Section does not preclude the use of other forms.

(1) For an individual acting in his own right:

State of ....
County of ....

The foregoing instrument was acknowledged before me this (date) by (name of person acknowledged.)

(Signature of person taking acknowledgment)
(Title or rank)
(Serial number, if any)

(2) For a corporation:

State of ....
County of ....
The foregoing instrument was acknowledged before me this (date) by (name of officer or agent, title of officer or agent) of (name of corporation acknowledging) a (state or place of incorporation) corporation, on behalf of the corporation.

(Signature of person taking acknowledgment)
(Title or rank)
(Serial number, if any)

(3) For a partnership:

State of ....
County of ....

The foregoing instrument was acknowledged before me this (date) by (name of acknowledging partner or agent), partner (or agent) on behalf of (name of partnership), a partnership.

(Signature of person taking acknowledgment)
(Title or rank)
(Serial number, if any)

(4) For an individual acting as principal by an attorney in fact:

State of ....
County of ....
The foregoing instrument was acknowledged before me this (date) by (name of attorney in fact) as attorney in fact on behalf of (name of principal).

(Signature of person taking acknowledgment)
(Title or rank)
(Serial number, if any)

(5) By any public officer, trustee, or personal representative:

State of ....
County of ....

The foregoing instrument was acknowledged before me this (date) by (name and title of position).

(Signature of person taking acknowledgment)

(Title or rank)
(Serial number, if any)

(b) This amendatory Act of 1981 (P.A. 82-450) is to clarify that any uses of the short form of acknowledgment as herein provided within the State of Illinois prior to the effective date of this amendatory Act have been valid.

History

P.A. 82-450; 90-655, § 181.

765 ILCS 30/8. Acknowledgments not affected by this Act.

A notarial act performed prior to the effective date of this Act is not affected by this Act. This Act provides an additional method of proving notarial acts. Nothing in this Act diminishes or invalidates the recognition accorded to notarial acts by other laws or regulations of this State.

History

P.A. 76-1105.

765 ILCS 30/9. Uniformity of interpretation.

This Act shall be so interpreted as to make uniform the laws of those states which enact it.

History

P.A. 76-1105.

765 ILCS 30/10. Time of taking effect.

This Act shall take effect on January 1, 1970.

History

P.A. 76-1105.

ACT 33. UNIFORM REAL PROPERTY ELECTRONIC RECORDING ACT

765 ILCS 33/3. Validity of electronic documents.

(a) If a law requires, as a condition for recording, that a document be an original, be on paper or another tangible medium, or be in writing, the requirement is satisfied by an electronic document satisfying this Act.

(b) If a law requires, as a condition for recording, that a document be signed, the requirement is satisfied by an electronic signature.

(c) A requirement that a document or a signature associated with a document be notarized, acknowledged, verified, witnessed, or made under oath is satisfied if the electronic signature of the person authorized to perform that act, and all other information required to be included, is attached to or logically associated with the document or signature. A physical or electronic image of a stamp, impression, or seal need not accompany an electronic signature.

History

P.A. 95-472, § 3.

5 ILCS 312/3.5. Electronic documents certified by notary public.

(a) A paper or tangible copy of an electronic document that a notary public has certified to be a true and correct copy under subsection (b) satisfies any requirement of law that, as a condition for recording, the document:

(1) be an original or be in writing;

(2) be signed or contain an original signature, if the document contains an electronic signature of the person required to sign the document; and

(3) be notarized, acknowledged, verified, witnessed, or made under oath, if the document contains an electronic signature of the person authorized to perform that act, and all other information required to be included.

(b) A notary public duly appointed and commissioned under Section 2-101 of the Illinois Notary Public Act may certify that a paper or tangible copy of an electronic document is a true and correct copy of the electronic document if the notary public has:

(1) reasonably confirmed that the electronic document is in a tamper evident format;

(2) detected no changes or errors in any electronic signature or other information in the electronic document;

(3) personally printed or supervised the printing of the electronic document onto paper or other tangible medium; or

(4) not made any changes or modifications to the electronic document or to the paper or tangible copy thereof other than the certification described in this subsection (b).

(c) A county recorder shall accept for recording a paper or tangible copy of a document that has been certified by a notary public to be a true and correct copy of an electronic document under subsection (b) as evidenced by a notarial certificate.

(d) A notarial certificate in substantially the following form is sufficient for the purposes of this Section:

"State of
County of

On this (date), I certify that the foregoing and annexed document [entitled ,] (and) containing pages is a true and correct copy of an electronic document printed by me or under my supervision. I further certify that, at the time of printing, no security features present on the electronic document indicated any changes or errors in an electronic signature or other information in the electronic document since its creation or execution.

(Signature of Notary Public)
(Seal)"

(f) If a notarial certificate is attached to or made a part of a paper or tangible document, the certificate is prima facie evidence that the requirements of subsection (c) have been satisfied with respect to the document.

(g) A paper or tangible copy of a deed, mortgage, or other document shall be deemed, from the time of being filed for record, as notice to subsequent purchasers and creditors, though it may not be certified in accordance with the provisions of this Section.

(h) This Section does not apply to any map or plat governed by the Plat Act, the Judicial Plat Act, or the Permanent Survey Act, or to any monument record governed by the Land Survey Monuments Act.

History

Contingently enacted by 2021 P.A. 102-160, § 25, effective January 1, 2022.

CHAPTER 815. BUSINESS TRANSACTIONS

ACT 815. UNIFORM ELECTRONIC TRANSACTIONS ACT

815 ILCS 333/11 Notarization and acknowledgment.

If a law requires a signature or record to be notarized, acknowledged, verified, or made under oath, the requirement is satisfied if the electronic signature of the person authorized to perform those acts, together with all other information required to be included by other applicable law, is attached to or logically associated with the signature or record.

History

2021 P.A. 102-38, § 11, effective June 25, 2021.

ILLINOIS ADMINISTRATIVE CODE

TITLE 14: COMMERCE
SUBTITLE A: REGULATION OF BUSINESS
CHAPTER I: SECRETARY OF STATE
PART 176
NOTARY PUBLIC RECORDS

SUBPART A: NOTARY PUBLIC RECORDS

Section

SUBPART B: APPOINTMENTS

Section

SUBPART C: COURSE OF STUDY AND EXAMINATION

Section

SUBPART D: NOTARY PUBLIC APPLICATION REQUIREMENTS

Section

SUBPART E: NOTARY PUBLIC REMITTANCE AGENT

Section

SUBPART F: DUTY, FEES, AUTHORITY

Section

SUBPART G: NOTARIAL ACTS

Section

176.600 Notarial Certificates

176.610 Persons Physically Unable to Sign Documents

SUBPART H: REMOTE NOTARIAL ACTS

Section

176.700 Standards for Remote Notarial Acts Using Audio-Video Communication

176.710 Remote Notarial Acts – Recording

176.720 Requirement to Restart Performance of Act Under Certain Circumstances

176.730 Remote Notarial Certificates

SUBPART I: ELECTRONIC NOTARIZATIONS

Section

176.800 Electronic Notary Public Commission Required

176.802 Definitions

176.805 Electronic Notarization System Provider Registration, Information Submitted for Registration, and Confidentiality of Certain Information

176.810 Information Required in Electronic Seal, Electronic Documents Made TamperEvident, and Notation Required if Audio-Video Communication Is Used to Perform Notarial Acts

176.815 Access and Use of Electronic Notary Seal and Electronic Signature

176.820 Changes to Digital Certificate and Electronic Seal of Electronic Notary

176.825 Standards for Communication Technology

176.830 Duties of Electronic Notary Public

176.835 Standards for Identity Verification

176.840 Maintenance of Record of Electronic Notarial Act

176.845 Electronic Notarial Act Using Audio-Video Communication – Duty of Electronic Notary and System Provider to Protect Recordings and Personally Identifying Information from Unauthorized Access

176.850 Use of System Provider to Store Electronic Journals and Recordings

176.855 Availability of Recordings and Documents to Certain Persons and Entities

176.860 Electronic Notarial Acts

176.865 Electronic Notarial Certificates

176.870 Prohibited Acts

SUBPART J: JOURNAL

Section

176.900 Journal Requirements

SUBPART K: ADMINISTRATIVE HEARINGS

Section

AUTHORITY: Implemented and authorized by Section 1-104 of the Illinois Notary Public Act [5 ILCS 312].

SOURCE: Adopted at 11 Ill. Reg. 19705, effective December 1, 1987; amended at 13 Ill. Reg. 5197, effective April 1, 1989; amended at 45 Ill. Reg. 6274, effective April 28, 2021; amended at 47 Ill. Reg.8640, effective June 5, 2023.

SUBPART A: NOTARY PUBLIC RECORDS

Section 176.10 Definitions

For purposes of this Section, all words and terms shall have the same meanings as set forth in 5 ILCS 312/1-104:

"Act" means The Illinois Notary Public Act. [5 ILCS 312]

"Biometric data" or "biometric identifier" means a retina or iris scan, fingerprint, voiceprint, or scan of hand or face geometry. Biometric identifiers do not include writing samples, written signatures, photographs, human biological samples used for valid scientific testing or screening, demographic data, tattoo descriptions, or physical descriptions such as height, weight, hair color, or eye color. Biometric identifiers do not include donated organs, tissues, or parts as defined in the Illinois Anatomical Gift Act or blood or serum stored on behalf of recipients or potential recipients of living or cadaveric transplants and obtained or stored by a federally designated organ procurement agency. Biometric identifiers do not include biological materials regulated under the Genetic Information Privacy Act. Biometric identifiers do not include information captured from a patient in a health care setting or information collected, used, or stored for health care treatment, payment or operations under the federal Health Insurance Portability and Accountability Act of 1996. Biometric identifiers do not include an X-ray, roentgen process, computed tomography, MRI, PET scan, mammography, or other image or film of the human anatomy used to diagnose, prognose, or treat an illness or other medical condition or to further validate scientific testing or screening. [740 ILCS 14/10]

"Biometric information" means any information, regardless of how it is captured, converted, stored, or shared, based on an individual's biometric identifier used to identify an individual. Biometric information does not include information derived from items or procedures excluded under the definition of biometric identifiers. [740 ILCS 14/10]

"Notary public" or "notary" means an individual commissioned to perform notarial acts. [5 ILCS 312/1-104]

"Personal information" or "personally identifiable information" means either of the following:

An individual's first name or first initial and last name in combination with any one or more of the following data elements, when either the name or the data elements are not encrypted or redacted or are encrypted or redacted but the keys to unencrypt or unredact or otherwise read the name or data elements have been acquired without authorization through the breach of security: Social Security number; Driver's license number or State identification card number; Account number or credit or debit card number, or an account number or credit card number in combination with any required security code, access code, or password that would permit access to an individual's financial account; Medical information; Health insurance information; Unique biometric data means data generated from measurements or technical analysis of human body characteristics used by the owner or licensee to authenticate an individual, such as a fingerprint, retina or iris image, or other unique physical representation or digital representation of biometric data. [815 ILCS 530/5] User name or email address means information provided in combination with a password or security question and answer that would permit access to an online account when either the user name or email address or password or security question and answer are not encrypted or redacted or are encrypted or redacted but the keys to unencrypt or unredact or otherwise read the data elements have been obtained through the breach of security.

"Personal information" does not include publicly available information that is lawfully made available to the general public from federal, State, or local government records. [815 ILCS 530/5]

"Physical location" means real property, non-movable structure, brick and mortar building affixed to a permanent location.

"Secretary" – means the Illinois Secretary of State.

"X.509" means the standard format of a public key certificate derived from the International Telecommunication Union, "Series X: Data Networks, Open System

Communications and Security Directory" (https://www.itu.int/rec/T-REC-X.509-201910-I) (2019) (no later editions or amendments included).

(Source: Added at 47 Ill. Reg. 8640, effective June 5, 2023)

Section 176.11 Record Contents, Request Procedures, and Fees

a) The Secretary maintains Illinois Notary Public appointment records in its computer database. The computer records contain the notary's name, address, city, state, zip code, county, commission number, and the date the commission took effect.

b) All requests for this information shall be in writing, signed before a notary by the person requesting the information. The request shall include the person's address, the purpose of the request, the specific information requested, the name and address of any organization represented by the requestor, and the position of the requestor in the organization. Approved requests shall be formalized in a written agreement.

c) All requests shall be accompanied by the appropriate fee and sent to the following address: Office of the Secretary of State, Index Department, 111 E. Monroe Street, Springfield, Illinois 62756.

d) A list of all current notaries or all notaries in a particular county will be furnished for a fee of $ 3,600. Weekly update lists will be furnished for $ 1,000 per year paid in advance. The fee for a list of notaries commissioned during a specific calendar year is $ 900 and the fee for a list of notaries commissioned during a specific month of a specific year is $ 75.

e) State, federal, and local law enforcement agencies will receive information at no charge if the information is needed for an official investigation. All other governmental agencies, including county clerks, will receive a list of all current notaries for a fee of $ 500 if requested for governmental purposes; weekly updates will be furnished for $ 1,000 per year paid in advance. A list of all notaries in one particular county will be furnished for a fee of $ 200 and weekly updates will be furnished for $ 500 per year paid in advance.

f) The fees shall be paid by cashier's check, money order, certified check, or a check drawn on the account of the business or government agency making the request. Once the information is made available to the requestor, then no refunds will be made.

g) Record layouts and field definitions will be supplied by the Secretary with the information.

(Source: Amended at 13 Ill. Reg. 5197, effective April 1, 1989; amended at 45 Ill. Reg. 6274, effective April 28, 2021.)

SUBPART B: APPOINTMENTS

Section 176.100 Appointment and Reappointment of Notaries Public

a) Every applicant for an initial appointment or reappointment as a notary public must present satisfactory evidence of the applicant's identity as set forth in the Act at 5 ILCS 312/2-102.

b) Before issuance of an appointment as a notary public or electronic notary public, the applicant for appointment must:

1) execute the oath of office as set forth at 5 ILCS 312/2-104;

2) submit a bond as set forth at 5 ILCS 312/2-105; and

3) complete all application requirements found at 5 ILCS 312/2-102(a) and, if applying for an electronic notary public commission, at 5 ILCS 312/2-102(c).

c) Upon a determination that an applicant meets all requirements of the Act and this Part, the Secretary of State will appoint or reappoint the applicant to the office of notary public or electronic notary public, as applicable, and issue a notary public or electronic notary public commission certificate.

d) Reappointment

1) A current notary public may apply for reappointment 60 days before the expiration of an existing commission. The date of the new commission will be the date immediately after the expiration date of the current commission.

2) To avoid any gaps between notary public or electronic notary public commissions, applications for a notary public should be filed at least 30 days before the expiration of the commission under which the notary public is acting.

e) Any applicant can request the cancellation of an appointment and the cancellation will become effective upon receipt by the Secretary of State of the notice requesting cancellation of the appointment.

(Source: Added at 47 Ill. Reg. 8640, effective June 5, 2023)

Section 176.110 Term of Commission

The term of a notary public or electronic notary public commission begins on the date that the notary is commissioned by the Secretary of State and not the date the bond was obtained. The electronic notary public commission, if any, will have the same term of commission as the traditional notary public commission.

(Source: Added at 47 Ill. Reg. 8640, effective June 5, 2023)

Section 176.120 Requirements to Qualify as a Resident of the State of Illinois

An applicant must be a resident of the State of Illinois pursuant to 5 ILCS 312/2-101 before applying for a notary public or electronic notary public commission, unless applying for a nonresident application or appointment pursuant to 5 ILCS 312/2-101 and Section 176.130. A notary public or electronic notary public must maintain residency in the State of Illinois during the term of the appointment and must immediately resign the notary public or electronic notary public commission if the notary public's residency in Illinois ends.

(Source: Added at 47 Ill. Reg. 8640, effective June 5, 2023)

Section 176.130 Nonresident Application for Appointment

The form in Illustration A must be used by an applicant for notary public who resides in a state bordering Illinois whose place of work or business is within a county in Illinois, but only if the laws of the applicant's state of residence authorize residents of Illinois to be appointed and commissioned as notaries public in that state. [5 ILCS 312/2-101(a)]

(Source: Added at 47 Ill. Reg. 8640, effective June 5, 2023)

SUBPART C: COURSE OF STUDY AND EXAMINATION

Section 176.200 Definitions

Unless otherwise noted, the following definitions apply to this Subpart only:

"Applicant" means a person or entity applying for certification as a notary public course of study provider and examination provider.

"Certification" means a document issued by the Department that authorizes the entity named in the document to offer a live classroom or webcast course of study and examination required by 5 ILCS 312/2-101.5.

"Consumer information" means the name, address, date of birth, email address and payment information, including credit card and bank account numbers or electronic payment data of students who are enrolled in or have completed a notary public course of study and examination.

"Department" means the Index Department of the Office of the Secretary of State.

"Instructor" means the person charged with providing instruction to notary applicants.

"Live certified proctors" means a person or persons who monitor students in real time in a live classroom setting.

"Multimedia" means a method or methods of technology meant to convey information including, but not limited to animation, graphics, and video displays.

"Provider" means an entity or person certified by the Secretary of State to provide a notary public course of study and examination required by 5 ILCS 312/2-101.5.

"Shareware" means copyrighted software for which the copyright owner sets certain conditions for the software's distribution and use, including requiring payment to the copyright owner after a person who has secured a copy of the software decides to use the software.

"Webcast" means either a live synchronous online or interactive asynchronous course of study and examination as required by 5 ILCS 312/2-101.5.

"Web video conference proctor" means a person or persons who monitor students in real time during a video conference and/or examination.

(Source: Added at 47 Ill. Reg. 8640, effective June 5, 2023)

Section 176.205 Course of Study and Examination

a) Beginning January 1, 2024, applicants seeking a commission as either a notary public or an electronic notary public must first successfully complete a course of study and acquire a passing score on the examination, as required by 5 ILCS 312/2-101.5. The applicant will have 2 years from the date of the examination to apply for a notary public or electronic notary public commission. Once the course of study and examination have been successfully completed and the commission has been issued, the certificate or other proof of successful completion of the course of study and examination will remain valid for the duration of the notary's four-year commission.

b) The Secretary of State may authorize the provision of a course of study for the mandatory training of notaries public and electronic notaries public by qualified third parties subject to this Subpart.

c) To be accepted by the Secretary, the course of study must be taught by a provider or instructor certified by the Secretary.

d) The course of study and examination must consist of the instruction and questions identified in Section 176.225.

(Source: Added at 47 Ill. Reg. 8640, effective June 5, 2023)

SUBPART D: NOTARY PUBLIC APPLICATION REQUIREMENTS

Section 176.300 Application for Notary Public and Electronic Notary Public Commissions

a) Applications for a traditional notary public commission. All individuals applying for a traditional notary public commission shall use the application prescribed by the Secretary of State and shall include, at a minimum, the information required by 5 ILCS 312/2-102.

b) Remote notarization. Any notary appointed under subsection (a) shall have the authority to conduct remote notarizations. [5 ILCS 312/2-102(b)]

c) Application for electronic notary public commission. An application for an electronic notary public commission must be filed with the Secretary of State as required by this Subpart D [5 ILCS 312/2-102(c)]. In addition, an applicant for an electronic notary public commission must provide the following:

1) The notary public commission number assigned to the person by the Secretary of State, unless the applicant is applying for the notary public commission and electronic notary public commission at the same time under 5 ILCS 312/2-101(c);

2) The names of all electronic notarization system providers that the applicant intends to use to perform electronic notarial acts;

3) A copy of the electronic signature of the person that is:

A) an exact representation of the handwritten signature of the person already on file or currently being filed with the Secretary of State; and

B) in a format that can be read without additional software and be compared for authentication purposes to the person's handwritten signature on file or being filed with the Secretary;

4) A statement certifying that the applicant:

A) Will comply with the standards set forth by Section 176.835 relating to identity proofing and credential analysis;

B) Will use a third-party provider who has been certified to act as an electronic notarization system provider in the State of Illinois by the Secretary; and

C) Will, upon request by the Secretary, promptly provide any necessary instructions or techniques supplied by a provider that will allow the electronic notary public's digital certificate and electronic seal to be read and authenticated.

5) A disclosure of all disciplinary actions, convictions, or administrative actions taken against the applicant;

6) A certificate or other proof of successful completion of the course of study required under 5 ILCS 312/2-101.5(a), which indicates successful completion of the course within the 2 years preceding the submission of the application for an electronic notary public commission; and

7) A statement certifying that the person will comply with the applicable provisions of the Act, including Article VI-A.

d) A person may not perform an electronic notarial act, unless:

1) The Secretary has approved the applicant's application for an electronic notary public commission; and

2) The Secretary has approved the registration of the proposed electronic notarization system provider.

e) Incomplete applications. If an application for appointment as a notary public or electronic notary public is incomplete, the Secretary of State will retain the application for at least 1 year from the date of receipt of the application. If the applicant does not complete the application within 1 year from the date of receipt of the application, the Secretary of State may deny the application and mail a notice of denial to the applicant.

f) Assignment of Commission Number.

1) The Secretary of State will assign a unique commission number to each original commission certificate. The commission number, which will be used to identify the notary public whose name appears on the commission certificate, must remain assigned to the notary public throughout the period of the appointment and must be included on each duplicate or amended commission certificate issued to the notary public by the Secretary of State.

2) If a notary public applies for a subsequent period of appointment, a new number must be assigned.

3) A notary public that is also commissioned as an electronic notary public will have the same commission number for both commissions.

g) After an application for an electronic notary public commission has been approved, the electronic notary public will be required to notify the Office of the Secretary of State, on a form designated by the Secretary, if the electronic notary public elects to add any other electronic notary system provider.

(Source: Added at 47 Ill. Reg. 8640, effective June 5, 2023)

Section 176.310 Approval of Application, Authority of Secretary of State to Deny Commission, and Effective Date of Commission

a) If an applicant who is applying for an electronic notary public commission satisfies all of the requirements for such a commission pursuant to this Part and 5 ILCS 312/2-102, the Secretary of State will:

1) Approve the application for a commission as an electronic notary;

2) Update the processing system maintained by the Office of the Secretary of State to indicate the commission of the person as an electronic notary; and

3) Notify the applicant of the approved application and commission as an electronic notary.

b) If a person who is applying for an electronic notary public commission does not meet all of the requirements for application set forth in this Part and 5 ILCS 312/2-101, the Secretary of State will not commission the person as an electronic notary public. If the Secretary of State denies a commission as an electronic notary under this sub-section, the Secretary of State will notify the person of that refusal.

c) The commission of a person as an electronic notary public becomes effective at the time the processing system maintained by the Secretary of State has been updated pursuant to subsection (a)(2) to indicate such a commission.

(Source: Added at 47 Ill. Reg. 8640, effective June 5, 2023)

Section 176.320 Appointment Fee

a) No commission will be issued until the fee required by 5 ILCS 312/2-103 has been paid in full.

b) Authority of the Secretary of State to deny or revoke commission if payment is dishonored or stopped. If any method of payment submitted by an applicant to the Secretary of State pursuant to 5 ILCS 312/2-103 is returned to the Secretary of State or otherwise dishonored upon presentation of payment because the applicant has insufficient money or credit, or because the person stopped payment on the method of payment, the Secretary of State may immediately and without a hearing deny to commission the applicant as a notary public or electronic notary public or immediately revoke the applicant's commission if the commission has already been granted. An applicant whose commission is denied or revoked under this subsection (b) must resubmit an application for commission as a notary public or electronic notary public.

A notary public or electronic notary public whose commission is revoked under this subsection (b) must reapply for a commission.

(Source: Added at 47 Ill. Reg. 8640, effective June 5, 2023)

Section 176.330 Oath

a) Notaries public and electronic notaries public must file an oath of office with the Secretary of State, affirming the notary's or electronic notary's intent to follow the laws and constitutions of the United States of America and the State of Illinois.

b) The legal name on the applicant's oath of office must exactly match the applicant's driver's license or state identification card and the name on the notary public application. Unless proven otherwise, the name shall consist of the applicant's first personal name (first name), additional name or names, if applicable, and surname (family or last name)

(Source: Added at 47 Ill. Reg. 8640, effective June 5, 2023)

Section 176.340 Bond

a) Applicants for a notary public commission or electronic notary public commission must indicate at the time of application whether the applicant will perform only traditional in-person notarizations or remote notarizations.

b) An applicant for a notary public commission or electronic notary public commission must purchase a bond in the following amounts:

1) Applicants seeking to perform only traditional, in-person notarizations – $5,000;

2) Applicants seeking to perform traditional, in-person notarizations and remote or electronic notarizations – $25,000 in addition to the bond required by subsection (b)(1) for traditional notaries, or a combined bond of $30,000, pursuant to 5 ILCS 312/2-105(b).

c) A copy of the original bond must be filed with the Illinois Secretary of State Index Department.

d) The bond shall contain, on its face, the oath of office for the notary public or electronic notary public as specified in 5 ILCS 312/2-104. The applicant must endorse the oath on the face of the bond, immediately below the oath, by signing the applicant's name under which the person has applied to be commissioned as a notary public or electronic notary public and exactly as it appears on the notary application form or electronic notary application form filed with the Secretary of State's Office.

e) In making a claim against a combined bond, as described in subsection (b)(2), a claimant will only be entitled to either a maximum of $5,000 of the bond if the notarization at question was a traditional, in-person, physical notarization or a maximum of $25,000 if the notarization was electronic or remote. In no event may a single claim be eligible for payment of the entirety of the $30,000 bond.

(Source: Added at 47 Ill. Reg. 8640, effective June 5, 2023)

Section 176.350 Reappointment

a) A current notary public and a current electronic notary public may apply for reappointment 60 days before an existing commission expires. The date of the new commission will be the date immediately after the expiration date of the current commission.

b) To prevent a gap between commissions, a notary public and electronic notary public should apply for reappointment at least 30 days before the commission under which the notary public is currently acting expires.

(Source: Added at 47 Ill. Reg. 8640, effective June 5, 2023)

SUBPART F: DUTY, FEES, AUTHORITY

Section 176.500 Use of Official Seal and Electronic Seal

a) A notary public must use the notary public's official seal, affixed using a rubber stamp, to perform a notarial act. An electronic notary public must use the electronic notary public's electronic seal, affixed using a mechanical stamp, to perform an electronic notarial act.

b) A notary public must place a legible imprint of the notary public's official seal on a notarial certificate for a tangible record at the time of the performance of the notarial act.

c) An electronic notary public must attach or logically associate the electronic notary public's electronic seal with the electronic notarial certificate on an electronic record.

d) A notary public must not place an imprint of the notary public's official seal, and an electronic notary public must not attach or logically associate the electronic notary public's electronic seal, over any signature in a record to be notarized or over any writing in a notarial certificate.

e) When a notarial certificate is on a separate piece of paper attached to the tangible record to be notarized, or when there are attachments to the tangible record to be notarized, a notary public may use one additional imprint of the notary public's official seal for identification of the tangible record and notarial certificate attached to the tangible record, if the imprint does not make any part of the record or attachment illegible. The additional seal must be partially stamped together on the notarial certificate, and on the signature page or attachment to the notarized record.

f) A notary public may not use the notary public's official seal, and an electronic notary public may not use the electronic notary public's electronic seal, for any purpose other than to perform a notarial act.

g) A notary public may not permit any other person to use the notary public's official seal, and an electronic notary public may not permit any other person to use the electronic notary public's electronic seal, for any purpose.

h) A notary public may not use any other notary public's official seal or any other object in place of the notary public's official seal to perform a notarial act.

i) An electronic notary public may not use any other electronic notary public's electronic seal or any other object in place of the electronic notary public's electronic seal to perform a notarial act.

(Source: Added at 47 Ill. Reg. 8640, effective June 5, 2023)

Section 176.510 Acquiring the Official Seal and the Electronic Seal

a) A notary public may purchase an official seal, and an electronic notary public may purchase an electronic seal, only after receiving a commission certificate from the Department under Section 176.550(a), and providing a copy of the commission certificate to the notary public's or electronic notary public's chosen seal vendor.

b) The official seal of a notary public, and the electronic seal of an electronic notary public, is the exclusive property of the notary public or electronic notary public and may not be surrendered to an employer upon termination of employment, regardless of whether the employer paid for the official seal or electronic seal, the bond, or the appointment fees.

(Source: Added at 47 Ill. Reg. 8640, effective June 5, 2023)

Section 176.520 Description of the Official Seal and Electronic Seal

a) The reasonably legible imprint of an official seal of a notary public must contain:

1) A serrated or milled edge border in a rectangular form not more than one inch in height by two and one-half inches in length surrounding the following information in descending order:

A) The words "Official Seal";

B) The notary's official name, printed;

C) The words "Notary Public, State of Illinois";

D) The words "Commission No." immediately followed by the notary public's commission number; an

E) The words "My Commission Expires", immediately followed by the notary public's commission expiration date, expressed in terms of the month, one- or two-digit day, and complete year (e.g., January 1, 2024). [5 ILCS 312/3-101(a)]

2) The imprint of an official seal of a notary public on a tangible record must be an imprint capable of being photocopied or reproduced.

b) The electronic seal of an electronic notary public on an electronic record must look identical to a traditional notary public seal and be accompanied by the electronic signature of the electronic notary public and language explicitly stating that the electronic notarial act was performed using audio-video communication, if applicable. [5 ILCS 312/3-101(b-5)].

c) A notary may continue to use any seal in effect before July 1, 2023 through the expiration of the notary's current commission.

d) If the notary's official seal appears illegible on the document, a notary public may reapply a second, or subsequent, official seal to the document. Application of a second or subsequent seal must not make any other portion of the document unreadable.

(Source: Added at 47 Ill. Reg. 8640, effective June 5, 2023)

Section 176.530 Replacement of Lost, Compromised, Destroyed, or Stolen Official Seal or Electronic Seal

a) When a physical official seal is lost or stolen, the notary public must notify the Department in writing the next business day after discovering the seal was lost or stolen. When an electronic official seal is lost or stolen, the notary public must notify the Department the next business day under 5 ILCS 312/3-101(d)(2).

b) A replacement official seal or electronic seal must contain a distinct difference from the original seal.

c) If the lost or stolen official or electronic seal is found or recovered after a replacement has been obtained, the original seal must be destroyed.

(Source: Added at 47 Ill. Reg. 8640, effective June 5, 2023)

Section 176.540 Notary Public and Electronic Notary Public Fees

a) A notary public or electronic notary public may charge the fees prescribed in 5 ILCS 312/3-104.

b) Neither a notary public nor an electronic notary public is required to charge a fee. A notary public or electronic notary public who charges a fee shall not charge more than the maximum fee allowed by 5 ILCS 312/3-104.

c) Before performing any notarial act, the notary public or electronic notary public must inform the requestor of the notary's or electronic notary's fee, if any, that will be charged.

d) A notary public or electronic notary public who advertises notarial services in a language other than English or performs services as described in 5 ILCS 312/3-103 must post a schedule of the fees listed in 5 ILCS 312/3-104 in a conspicuous location at all times, as required by 5 ILCS 312/3-103(b).

(Source: Added at 47 Ill. Reg. 8640, effective June 5, 2023)

Section 176.550 Commission Certificate

a) Upon appointment as a notary public or electronic notary public, the Secretary of State shall send a commission certificate to the person appointed as a notary public or electronic notary public, with which the person appointed may obtain an official seal or electronic seal.

b) Only upon presentation by the notary public or electronic notary public of the Commission Certificate is a vendor authorized to provide the notary with an official seal described in Section 176.520 or an electronic notary with an electronic seal as described in Sections 176.520 and 176.810.

(Source: Added at 47 Ill. Reg. 8640, effective June 5, 2023)

SUBPART G: NOTARIAL ACTS

Section 176.600 Notarial Certificates

a) Minimum requirements. For a notarial certificate to be sufficient, it must contain the information required under 5 ILCS 312/6-103.

b) Additional Information. A notarial certificate may contain additional or other information as may be required to satisfy any legal requirements, ethical or legal concerns, or the business needs of the parties to the transaction.

c) Permanently and Securely Attached. A notarial certificate must be stamped, stapled, grommeted, or otherwise permanently bound to the tangible document in a tamper-evident manner. The use of tape, paper clips, or binder clips is not permitted.

d) Legible Signature Required. When signing a paper certificate, the notary public shall use a legible, recognizable handwritten signature that can be attributed to the notary public performing the notarial act by anyone examining or authenticating the signature. If a notary public's preferred signature is not legible and recognizable, the notary public must also legibly print the notary public's name immediately adjacent to the signature. In this chapter, a signature is legible and recognizable if the letters are distinct and easily readable, and the notary public's full name may be clearly discerned by looking at the signature.

(Source: Added at 47 Ill. Reg. 8640, effective June 5, 2023)

Section 176.610 Persons Physically Unable to Sign Documents

a) If a person cannot physically sign a document that is presented to a notary public and directs a person other than the notary to sign the person's name on the document, both the person who cannot physically sign the document and the person directed to sign the person's name on the document shall appear before the notary and be identified under 5 ILCS 312/6-102(d), 6-102.5(a), or 6A-103(b), as applicable, at the time the document is signed.

b) A notary public who performs a notarial act for a person who cannot physically sign shall type, print, or stamp the following, or a substantially similar statement, near the signature "Signature affixed by (name of individual) at the direction of (name of person physically unable to sign) in accordance with 14 Ill. Adm. Code 176.610".

(Source: Added at 47 Ill. Reg. 8640, effective June 5, 2023)

SUBPART H: REMOTE NOTARIAL ACTS

Section 176.700 Standards for Remote Notarial Acts Using Audio-Video Communication

a) Pursuant to Section 3-107 of the Act, a notary performing a remote notarization shall maintain an accurate and reliable record of each remote notarial act performed by the notary public.

b) Before performing a remote notarial act using audio-video communication, a remote notary public must confirm the identity of the remotely located principal by:

1) Personal knowledge;

2) The oath of a credible witness who personally knows the remotely located principal and who is personally known to the remote notary public; or

3) Remote presentation by the remotely located principal of a governmentissued identification credential that contains a photograph and the signature of the remotely located principal and otherwise conforms to the requirements of 5 ILCS 312/6-102.5(a)(3).

c) If a remote notary public can neither determine that a credential presented by a remotely located principal is a valid identification of the remotely located principal nor match the physical features of the remotely located principal with the credential presented by the remotely located principal, the remote notary public must not take any further action to complete a remote notarial act by using that credential to confirm the identity of the remotely located principal.

d) A remote notary public may perform a remote notarial act using audio-video communication only if the remote notary public and the remotely located principal agree to the performance of the remote notarial act using audio-video communication.

e) Standards for Audio-Video Communication Technology.

1) Communication technology, as defined in 5 ILCS 312/1-104, must provide synchronous audio-video feeds of sufficient video resolution and audio clarity to enable the remote notary public and remotely located principal to see and speak with each other. The process must provide a means for the remote notary public reasonably to confirm that a record presented for a notarial act is the same record in which the remotely located principal made a statement or on which the principal executed a signature.

2) A remote notary public performing a remote notarial act using audio-video communication must verify that the communication technology is sufficient to protect the act and the recording of the act made under Section 176.710 and that any personally identifiable information disclosed during the performance of the remote notarial act is protected from unauthorized access, except as may be required to comply with the Act and Section 176.710(d), including unauthorized access to:

A) the live transmission of the audio-video feeds;

B) the methods used to perform identity verification; and

C) the recorded audio-video communication that is the subject of the remote notarization.

f) If a remotely located principal must exit the workflow before completing the identity verification process, the remotely located principal must restart the identity verification process from the beginning.

g) A remote notary public performing a remote notarization must identify a remotely located principal using the means specified in 5 ILCS 312/6-102.5(a). Nothing in this Part shall prohibit a remote notary public from using enhanced identity verification. (i.e., dynamic knowledge-based assessments).

(Source: Added at 47 Ill. Reg. 8640, effective June 5, 2023)

Section 176.710 Remote Notarial Acts – Recording

a) A notary public in the State of Illinois may perform a remote notarial act for remotely located principals under 5 ILCS 312/6-102.5

b) A remotely located principal may comply with the requirement to appear personally before a remote notary public by appearing remotely before the remote notary public using audio-video technology.

c) A remote notary public has satisfactory evidence of the identity of a remotely located principal if the remote notary public has personal knowledge of the identity of the remotely located principal or if the remote notary public has satisfactory evidence of the identity of the remotely located principal by oath or affirmation of a credible witness.

1) Personal Knowledge. A remote notary public has personal knowledge of the identity of the remotely located principal appearing before the remote notary public if the remotely located principal is personally known to the remote notary public through dealings sufficient to provide reasonable certainty that the remotely located principal has the identity claimed.

2) Credible Witness. To be a credible witness under Section 6-102.5(a)(3) of the Act, the witness shall have personal knowledge of the remotely located principal who has made a statement in or executed a signature on the record that is the subject of the remote notarial act. The remote notary public must have personal knowledge of the credible witness or shall have verified the identity of the credible witness. A credible witness may be a remotely located principal if the remote notary public, credible witness, and remotely located principal whose statement or signature is the subject of the notarial act can communicate by using audio-video technology.

3) Identity Verification. Remote presentation by a remotely located principal of a government-issued identification credential that contains a photograph and the signature of the remotely located principal and otherwise conforms to the requirements of 5 ILCS 312/6-102.5(a)(3).

d) The recording of a remote notarial act performed using audio-video communication, as required by this Part, must be made available upon request to the following persons or entities:

1) To the remotely located principal for whom the remote notarial act was performed;

2) To the Secretary of State;

3) To a law enforcement or federal, state, or local governmental agency in the course of an enforcement action or the performance of any lawful duty;

4) Pursuant to a court order or subpoena;

5) To the remote notary public who performed the remote notarial act;

6) To the employer of the remote notary public to ensure compliance with this Part or the Act; or

7) To any other person who is authorized to obtain the recording by the remotely located principal to the remote notarial act.

(Source: Added at 47 Ill. Reg. 8640, effective June 5, 2023)

Section 176.720 Requirement to Restart Performance of Act Under Certain Circumstances

a) A remote notary public who is performing a remote notarial act using audio-video communication must restart the performance of the remote notarial act from the beginning, including and without limitation confirming the identity of the remotely located principal in accordance with Section 176.700, if at any time during the performance of the remote notarial act:

1) The remotely located principal or the remote notary public exits the session;

2) The audio-video communication link is broken; or

3) The remote notary public believes that the process of completing the remote notarial act has been compromised and cannot be completed, for any reason, including poor resolution or quality of the audio or video transmission, or both.

b) As used in this Section, "session" means the performance of one or more remote notarial acts using audio-video communication on a single set of documents as a single event by a single remote notary public with one or more remotely located principals and any applicable witnesses.

(Source: Added at 47 Ill. Reg. 8640, effective June 5, 2023)

Section 176.730 Remote Notarial Certificates

a) A form of notarial certificate for a remote notarization complies with Sections 6-103 and 6-105 of the Act if it is in the form provided by applicable law and contains a statement substantially as follows: "This remote notarization involved the use of audio-video technology".

b) A short form of acknowledgment prescribed in 5 ILCS 312/6-105 or other form of notarial certificate required by law complies with 5 ILCS 312/6-103 if it follows substantially one of the forms in this subsection (b):

1) For an acknowledgment in an individual capacity:

> State of Illinois
> County of _____
>
> The foregoing instrument was acknowledged before me using audio-video technology on (date)_____ by _____(name(s) of individual(s))_____.
>
> (Signature of notary public)
> Notary Public
> (Notary seal)
> (My commission expires: _____)

2) For an acknowledgment in a representative capacity:

> State of Illinois
> County of _____
>
> The foregoing instrument was acknowledged before me using audio-video technology on (date) _____ by _____ (name(s) of individual(s)) _____ as (type of authority, such as officer or trustee) of (name of party on behalf of whom the instrument was executed).
>
> (Signature of notary public)
> Notary Public
> (Notary seal)
> (My commission expires: _____)

3) For a verification on an oath or affirmation:

> State of Illinois
> County of _____

Signed and sworn to (or affirmed) before me using audio-video technology on (date) _____ by _____ (name(s) of individual(s)) _____ making statement).

(Signature of notary public)
Notary public
(Notary seal)
(My commission expires: _____)

(Source: Added at 47 Ill. Reg. 8640, effective June 5, 2023)

SUBPART I: ELECTRONIC NOTARIZATIONS

Section 176.800 Electronic Notary Public Commission Required

a) A person may not perform an electronic notarial act unless the Secretary of State has approved the electronic notary public commission of a person under 5 ILCS 312/2-102 and the traditional notary public commission is in effect.

b) The Secretary of State may suspend or revoke the commission of a notary public who performs or offers to perform an electronic notarial act without an electronic notary public commission that has been approved by the Secretary of State, as required by Section 176.980(b).

(Source: Added at 47 Ill. Reg. 8640, effective June 5, 2023)

Section 176.802 Definitions

Unless otherwise noted, the following definitions apply to this Subpart I: "Electronic notarization system" or "system" means any combination of technology that enables a notary public to perform a notarial act remotely; that allows the notary public to communicate by sight and sound with the principal or witnesses, if applicable, using audio-video communication; and that includes features to conduct credential analysis and identity proofing.

"Electronic notarization system provider" or "provider" means the third-party vendor that operates, maintains, and sells access to an electronic notarization system. Providers may be manufacturers of the system, authorized representatives of a manufacturer, or other business entities.

(Source: Added at 47 Ill. Reg. 8640, effective June 5, 2023)

Section 176.810 Information Required in Electronic Seal, Electronic Documents Made Tamper-Evident, and Notation Required if Audio-Video Communication Is Used to Perform Notarial Acts

a) The electronic seal of an electronic notary public must have the information required to be included in an official seal under Section 176.520 and 5 ILCS 312/3-101(a) and must generally conform to the size and other requirements in Section 176.520 and 5 ILCS 312/3-101(a) and (b-5).

b) After the electronic seal and electronic signature are affixed or attached to or logically associated with an electronic notarial certificate of an electronic document and the electronic notarial act is thereby made complete, the electronic seal and electronic signature of the notary public must be capable of independent verification and the electronic document must be rendered tamper-evident.

c) If an electronic notary public performs an electronic notarial act using audiovideo communication, the electronic notary public must include adjacent to the electronic seal or in the electronic notarial certificate a notation indicating that the electronic notarial act was performed using audio-video communication. The notation required by this subsection must be the following statement or a substantially similar statement: "Notarial act performed by audio-video communication"

(Source: Added at 47 Ill. Reg. 8640, effective June 5, 2023)

Section 176.815 Access and Use of Electronic Notary Seal and Electronic Signature

a) Neither the employer of an electronic notary public nor any of the employer's employees or agents shall use or permit the use of an electronic notary seal or signature by anyone other than the authorized electronic notary public to whom it is registered.

b) Access to electronic notary signatures and electronic notary seals must be protected using biometric authentication, password authentication, token authentication, or other form of authentication approved by the Secretary according to the Act and this Part.

c) Report of Theft or Vandalism

1) An electronic notary public must report, in writing to the Secretary, the theft or vandalism of the notary's electronic signature, electronic notary seal, electronic record or journal, including the backup record, backup journal, and audio-video recordings within the next business day after discovering the theft or vandalism.

2) Failure to report the theft or vandalism is grounds for revocation of an electronic notary public's commission.

(Source: Added at 47 Ill. Reg. 8640, effective June 5, 2023)

Section 176.820 Changes to Digital Certificate and Electronic Seal of Electronic Notary

a) An electronic notary public shall at all times maintain an electronic seal and at least one digital certificate that includes the electronic notary's electronic signature. Both the electronic seal and digital certificate must comply with the Act and this Part.

b) An electronic notary may use more than one digital certificate in accordance with this Part.

c) An electronic notary public shall replace an electronic seal or digital certificate under the following circumstances:

1) The electronic seal or digital certificate has expired;

2) The electronic seal or digital certificate has been revoked or terminated by the device's issuing or registering authority; or

3) The electronic seal or digital certificate is for any reason no longer valid or capable of authentication.

d) An electronic notary public who replaces an electronic seal or digital certificate must provide the following to the Secretary of State within 10 days after the replacement:

1) The electronic technology or technologies to be used in attaching or logically associating the new electronic seal or digital certificate to an electronic document;

2) The electronic notary's new digital certificate, if applicable;

3) A copy of the electronic notary's new electronic seal, if applicable; and

4) Any necessary instructions or techniques supplied by the vendor that allow the electronic notary's electronic seal or digital certificate to be read and authenticated.

e) Digital certificates used by an electronic notary shall conform to the X.509 standard to ensure that the document has been rendered tamper-evident.

(Source: Added at 47 Ill. Reg. 8640, effective June 5, 2023)

Section 176.825 Standards for Communication Technology

a) Communication technology must provide synchronous audio-video feeds of sufficient video resolution and audio clarity to enable the electronic notary public and the individual to see and speak with each other in real time. The process must provide a means for the electronic notary reasonably to confirm that an electronic record before the electronic notary public is the same record in which the individual made a statement or on which the individual executed a signature.

b) Communication technology must provide reasonable security measures to prevent unauthorized access to:

1) The live transmission of the audio-video feeds;

2) The methods used to perform identity verification;

3) The electronic record that is the subject of the electronic notarization; and

4) Any electronic notary public's journal or audio-video recordings maintained or stored as a function of the communication technology.

c) If an individual must exit the workflow before completing the identity verification process, the individual must restart the identity verification process from the beginning.

(Source: Added at 47 Ill. Reg. 8640, effective June 5, 2023)

Section 176.830 Duties of Electronic Notary Public

An electronic notary public must take reasonable steps to:

a) Ensure the integrity, security, and authenticity of each electronic notarial act performed by the electronic notary public;

b) Maintain a secure backup of the electronic journal kept in accordance with 5 ILCS 312/3-107; and

c) Ensure that any audio-video communication while performing an electronic notarial act, and any journal records and audio-video recordings stored as a function of the communication technology, are secure from unauthorized access or interception.

(Source: Added at 47 Ill. Reg. 8640, effective June 5, 2023)

Section 176.835 Standards for Identity Verification

a) If an electronic notary public does not have satisfactory evidence of the identity of a remotely located principal pursuant to 5 ILCS 312/6A-103(b)(1), the electronic notary public must reasonably verify the principal's identity through a multifactor authentication procedure as provided in this Section. The procedure must analyze the principal's identification credential presented remotely against trusted third-person data sources, bind the principal's identity following a successful dynamic knowledge-based authentication assessment, and permit the electronic notary public to visually compare the identification credential and the principal. Credential analysis and identity proofing must be performed by a reputable third party who has provided evidence to the electronic notary public of the ability to comply with this Section.

b) Credential analysis must use public or private data sources to confirm the validity of the identification credential presented electronically by a principal and will, at a minimum:

1) Use automated software processes to aid the electronic notary public in verifying the identity of each principal;

2) Require the identification credential to pass an authenticity test, consistent with

sound commercial practices, that uses appropriate technologies to confirm the integrity of visual, physical, or cryptographic security features and to confirm that the identification credential is not fraudulent or inappropriately modified;

3) Use information held or published by the issuing source or an authoritative source, as available and consistent with sound commercial practices, to confirm the validity of personal details and identification credentials; and

4) Enable the electronic notary public to visually compare for consistency the information and photograph on the identification credential and the principal as viewed by the electronic notary public in real time through communication technology.

c) Identity proofing must be performed using a dynamic knowledge-based authentication assessment. The assessment is successful if it meets the following requirements:

1) The principal must answer a quiz consisting of a minimum of five questions related to the principal's personal history or identity formulated from public or private data sources;

2) Each question must have a minimum of five possible answer choices;

3) At least 80% of the questions must be answered correctly;

4) All questions must be answered within two minutes;

5) If the principal fails the first attempt, the principal may retake the quiz one time within 24 hours;

6) During a retake of the quiz, a minimum of 40% of the prior questions must be replaced;

7) If the principal fails the second attempt, the principal is not allowed to retry with the same electronic notary public within 24 hours of the second failed attempt; and

8) The electronic notary public must not be able to see or record the questions or answers.

d) An electronic notary public has satisfactory evidence of the identity of the principal if:

1) The electronic notary public has personal knowledge of the identity of the principal; or

2) The requirements of 5 ILCS 312/6A-103(b)(2) are satisfied.

(Source: Added at 47 Ill. Reg. 8640, effective June 5, 2023)

Section 176.840 Maintenance of Record of Electronic Notarial Act

Pursuant to 5 ILCS 312/3-107, an electronic notary public shall maintain an accurate and reliable journal record of each electronic notarial act performed by the electronic notary public. The record must be maintained for at least 7 years and must be made available to the Secretary upon request.

(Source: Added at 47 Ill. Reg. 8640, effective June 5, 2023)

Section 176.845 Electronic Notarial Act Using Audio-Video Communication – Duty of Electronic Notary and System Provider to Protect Recordings and Personally Identifying Information from Unauthorized Access

An electronic notary public performing an electronic notarial act using audio-video communication, and the provider whose system is used, must ensure that the recording of the electronic notarial act made under 5 ILCS 312/6A-104 and any personally identifiable information disclosed during the performance of the electronic notarial act is protected from unauthorized access.

(Source: Added at 47 Ill. Reg. 8640, effective June 5, 2023)

Section 176.850 Use of System Provider to Store Electronic Journals and Recordings

a) An electronic notary public may use a system provider to store the electronic journal of the electronic notary public and the recording made under 5 ILCS 312/6A-104 of an electronic notarial act performed using audio-video communication if the provider has registered with the Secretary of State and the provider's certification is in effect.

b) Except as otherwise provided in this subsection, a provider that stores the electronic journal of an electronic notary public and the recording made under 5 ILCS 312/6A-104 of an electronic notarial act performed using audio-video communication must allow the electronic notary public sole control of the electronic journal and the recording. The provider may allow access to the electronic journal of an electronic notary public or a recording if the electronic notary public has authorized such access or the access to the electronic journal or recording is authorized by the Act or this Part.

(Source: Added at 47 Ill. Reg. 8640, effective June 5, 2023)

Section 176.855 Availability of Recordings and Documents to Certain Persons and Entities

The recording made under 5 ILCS 312/6A-104 of an electronic notarial act performed using audio-video communication may be made available:

a) To the principal for whom the electronic notarial act was performed;

b) To the Secretary of State;

c) To a law enforcement or federal, state, or local governmental agency in the course of an enforcement action;

d) Pursuant to a court order or subpoena;

e) To the electronic notary public who performed the electronic notarial act for any purpose listed in subsections (a) through (d), inclusive;

f) To any other person who is authorized by the parties to the electronic notarial act to obtain the recording; or

g) For any authorized purpose and to ensure compliance with the provisions of this Part and Article VI-A of the Act governing electronic notarial acts, the employer of an electronic notary public who performs an electronic notarial act using audiovideo communication or the provider whose system was used to perform such an electronic notarial act, or both, may access the recording made under 5 ILCS 312/6A-104 of the electronic notarial act.

(Source: Added at 47 Ill. Reg. 8640, effective June 5, 2023)

Section 176.860 Electronic Notarial Acts

a) An electronic notary public may perform an electronic notarial act using audio-video communication only if the electronic notary public and the principal agree to the performance of the electronic notarial act using audio-video communication at the outset of the electronic notarization and before the identity of the principal has been confirmed.

b) Before performing an electronic notarial act using audio-video communication, an electronic notary public must confirm that the electronic document that is the subject of the electronic notarial act is the same document on which the principal made a statement or executed a signature and the identity of the principal. The identity of the principal shall be confirmed by:

1) Personal knowledge;

2) The oath of a credible witness who personally knows the principal and the notary public; or

3) Each of the following:

A) Remote presentation by the principal of a government-issued identification credential that contains a photograph and the signature of the principal;

B) Credential analysis of the government-issued credential and the data on the credential that complies with 5 ILCS 312/6A-103; and

C) A dynamic knowledge-based authentication assessment that complies with 5 ILCS 312/6A-103 or identity proofing under 5 ILCS 312/6A-103.

c) If an electronic notary public cannot determine that a credential presented by a principal is a valid identification of the principal or cannot match the physical features of the principal with the credential presented by the principal, the electronic notary public must not take any further action to complete an electronic notarial act by using that credential.

d) An electronic notary public who is performing an electronic notarial act using audio-video communication must restart from the beginning, including, without limitation, confirming the identity of the principal, if, at any time during the performance of the electronic notarial act:

1) The principal or the electronic notary public exits the session;

2) The audio-video communication link is broken; or

3) The electronic notary public believes that the process of completing the electronic notarization has been compromised and cannot be completed because of the resolution or quality of the audio or video transmission, or both.

e) An electronic notarial act will have the same force and effect as a notarial act performed in the physical presence of a notary public.

(Source: Added at 47 Ill. Reg. 8640, effective June 5, 2023)

Section 176.865 Electronic Notarial Certificates

a) A form of notarial certificate for an electronic notarization complies with 5 ILCS 312/6A-105 if it is in the form provided by applicable law and contains a statement substantially as follows: "This electronic notarization involved the use of an electronic system provider".

b) A short form of acknowledgment prescribed in 5 ILCS 312/6A-105 or other form of notarial certificate required by law complies with the Act if it is in substantially the same form as one of the following statements:

1) For an acknowledgment in an individual capacity:

> State of Illinois
> County of
>
> The foregoing instrument was acknowledged before me using an electronic notarization system provider on (date) by (name(s) of individual(s)).
>
> (Signature of notary public)
> Notary Public
> (Electronic seal)
> (My commission expires:)

2) For an acknowledgment in a representative capacity:

State of Illinois
County of

The foregoing instrument was acknowledged before me using an electronic notarization system provider on (date) by (name(s) of individual(s)) as (type of authority, such as officer or trustee) of (name of party on behalf of whom the instrument was executed).

(Signature of notary public)
Notary Public
(Electronic seal)
(My commission expires:)

3) For a verification on oath or affirmation:

State of Illinois
County of:
Signed and sworn to (or affirmed) before me using an electronic notarization system provider on (date) by (name(s) of individual(s) making statement).

(Signature of notary public)
Notary public
(Electronic seal)
(My commission expires:)

4) For witnessing or attesting a signature:

State of Illinois
County of:

Signed or attested before me on (date) by (name(s) of persons(s))

(Signature of notary public)
(Electronic seal)
(My commission expires:)

(Source: Added at 47 Ill. Reg. 8640, effective June 5, 2023)

Section 176.870 Prohibited Acts

a) An electronic notary public shall not:

1) Engage in any fraudulent activity, deceptive practice, or inequitable act in connection with the Act.

2) Engage in any activity prohibited by 5 ILCS 312/6-104.

3) Fail to record an electronic notarial act performed using audio-video communication or fail to keep such a recording as required by 5 ILCS 312/6A-104.

4) Use an electronic seal or digital certificate that is invalid or fails to comply with this Subpart or Article VI-A of the Act during the performance of an electronic notarial act.

5) Fail to notify the Secretary of State of a change in the electronic seal or digital certificate.

6) Use one's own electronic seal, alone or together with the electronic signature, except in the performance of an electronic notarial act.

7) Allow unauthorized access to the electronic journal kept by the electronic notary public under 5 ILCS 312/3-107, the electronic notary public's electronic signature or the digital certificate, or to the electronic notarization solution used by the electronic notary public to perform an electronic notarial act.

8) Violate any other provision of this Subpart I or Article VI-A of the Act relating to the performance of an electronic notarial act.

b) The penalties, prohibitions, liabilities, sanctions, and remedies for the improper performance of an electronic notarial act are the same as provided by law for the improper performance of a notarial act that is not an electronic notarial act.

(Source: Added at 47 Ill. Reg. 8640, effective June 5, 2023)

SUBPART J: JOURNAL

Section 176.900 Journal Requirements

a) Every notary public, whether or not also an electronic notary public, must record each notarial act in a journal at the time of notarization to comply with 5 ILCS 312/3-107 and this Subpart J.

b) Each journal of a notary public, whether maintained on a tangible medium or in an electronic format, must contain all of the following information in any order:

1) The name of the notary public as it appears on the commission;

2) The notary public's commission number;

3) The notary public's commission expiration date;

4) The notary public's office address of record with the Secretary of State;

5) A statement that, upon the death or adjudication of incompetency of the notary public, the notary public's personal representative or guardian or any other person knowingly in possession of the journal must deliver or mail it to the Secretary of State;

6) The meaning of any abbreviated word or symbol used in recording a notarial act in the notarial journal; and

7) The signature of the notary public.

c) If a notary public's name, commission expiration date, or address changes before the notary public stops using the notarial journal, the notary public shall add the new information after the old information and the date on which the information changed.

d) An electronic journal kept by a notary public or an electronic notary public under 5 ILCS 312/3-107 must comply with the requirements of subsections (a) and (b) and must also:

1) Prohibit the electronic notary public or any other person from deleting a record included in the electronic journal or altering the content or sequence of such a record after the record is entered into the electronic journal except to redact personally identifiable information as required by Section 176.910(d);

2) Be securely backed up by the electronic notary public and the electronic notarization system provider whose electronic notarization system was used by the electronic notary, if applicable; and

3) Omit all personally identifiable information, as defined in Section 176.10.

e) A notary public shall allow for the inspection of the journal or electronic journal as required by Section 176.950.

f) Notwithstanding any other subsection of this Part to the contrary, a notary employed by an attorney or law firm is not required to keep a journal of notarizations performed during the notary's employment if the attorney or law firm maintains a copy of the documents notarized. No attorney or law firm shall be required to violate attorney-client privilege by allowing or authorizing inspection of any notarizations that are recorded in a notary's journal. Journals of notarizations performed solely within the course of a notary's employment with an attorney or law firm are the property of the employing attorney or firm.

(Source: Added at 47 Ill. Reg. 8640, effective June 5, 2023)

Section 176.910 Journal Entries and Prohibited Entries

a) Required Entries. Each entry shall contain at least the following information:

1) The name of the principal;

2) The name of each credible witness relied upon to verify the identity of the principal;

3) The name of any other person that signed for the principal;

4) The title or a description of the document notarized;

5) The date of the notarization;

6) Whether the notarization was conducted in person, remotely, or electronically;

7) The fee charged, if any; and

8) The physical location of the notary and the principal.

b) Optional Entries. In addition to the entries required under 5 ILCS 312/3-107 of the Act and this Part, a journal may contain the signature of the individual for whom the notarial act is performed and any additional information about a specific transaction that might assist the notary public to recall the transaction.

c) Prohibited Entries. A notary public must not record in the notary's journal the following:

1) An identification number that was assigned by a governmental agency or by the United States to the principal that is set forth on the identification card or passport presented as identification;

2) Any other number that could be used to identify the principal of the document;

3) A biometric identifier, including a fingerprint, voice print, or retina image of the principal;

4) An individual's first name or first initial and last name in combination with and linked to any one or more of the following data elements when the data elements are not encrypted or redacted:

A) Social Security number;

B) Driver's license number or a State identification card number; or

C) Financial account information; and

5) An electronic signature of the person for whom an electronic notarial act was performed or any witnesses. [5 ILCS 312/3-107]

d) Inadvertent or Accidental Entries. A notary public who inadvertently records information prohibited under subsection (c) must redact such information before providing public access to or copies of the journal.

e) Fees. Each notarial fee charged should correspond to the notarial act performed. If a fee is waived or not charged, the notary public shall indicate so in the journal entry using notarizations such as "n/c", "0" (zero), or " – " (dash). Clerical and administrative fees, if charged, shall be separately itemized in the journal.

f) Address. For journal entries, address means the city and state only.

g) Transitional Provision. A notary public who holds a commission on July 1, 2023, may continue to use the notary public's journal until the completion of that journal or the expiration of that commission, whichever may occur first

(Source: Added at 47 Ill. Reg. 8640, effective June 5, 2023)

Section 176.920 Form and Content of Journals Maintained on a Tangible Medium

a) A journal maintained on paper or any other tangible medium may be in any form that meets the physical requirements in this Section and the entry requirements in Section 176.910.

b) The cover and pages inside the journal must be bound together by any binding method that is designed to prevent the insertion, removal, or substitution of the cover or a page. This includes glue, staples, grommets, or another binding, but does not include the use of tape, paper clips, or binder clips.

c) Each page must be consecutively numbered from the beginning to the end of the journal. If a journal provides two pages on which to record the required information about the same notarial act, both pages may be numbered with the same number or each page may be numbered with a different number. Page numbers must be preprinted.

d) Each line, or entry if the journal is designed with numbered entry blocks, must be consecutively numbered from the beginning to the end of the page. If a line extends across two pages, the line must be numbered with the same number on both pages. A line or entry number must be preprinted.

e) The journal of a notary public must remain within the exclusive control of the notary public at all times.

f) A notary public who performs multiple notarizations for the same principal within a single transaction may abbreviate the entry of those notarizations in the notary journal after first including all the information required by the Act. The abbreviated entry must indicate the type of transaction and the number of documents notarized as part of that single transaction.

g) A journal maintained in a tangible format must be retained for a minimum of 7 years after the final notarial act chronicled in the journal.

h) The retention requirements for this Part do not apply to notaries in the course of their employment with a governmental entity.

(Source: Added at 47 Ill. Reg. 8640, effective June 5, 2023)

Section 176.930 Form and Content of an Electronic Notarial Journal

a) A journal maintained in electronic format may be in any form that complies with this Section and the entry requirements in Section 176.910.

b) A journal maintained in an electronic format must be designed to prevent the insertion, removal, or substitution of an entry.

c) A journal maintained in an electronic format must be securely stored and recoverable in the case of a hardware or software malfunction.

d) Entries from the notarial journal must be available upon request by the Secretary of State in a PDF format.

e) The journal of a notary public shall remain within the exclusive control of the notary public at all times.

f) A notary public who performs multiple notarizations for the same principal within a single transaction may abbreviate the entry of those notarizations in the notary journal after first including all of the information required by the Act. The abbreviated entry must indicate the type of transaction and the number of documents notarized as part of that single transaction.

(Source: Added at 47 Ill. Reg. 8640, effective June 5, 2023)

Section 176.940 Custody and Control of the Journal and Notification of a Lost, Compromised, Destroyed, or Stolen Journal

a) The notary public must maintain custody and control of the journal at all times during the term of the notary public's commission. When not in use, the journal must be kept in a secure location and accessible only to the notary public. A secure location includes the notary public's sole possession or a locked location to which only the notary public has access.

b) Notification of a lost, compromised, destroyed, or stolen journal under 5 ILCS 312/3-107 must be made in writing or electronically the next business day after the date the notary public or personal representative or guardian discovers the loss or theft of the journal. The notification must include all of the following:

1) A statement of whether the journal is lost, compromised, destroyed, or stolen;

2) An explanation of how the journal became lost, compromised, destroyed, or stolen;

3) The date the notary public discovered that the journal was lost, compromised, destroyed, or stolen;

4) A statement that the journal has been destroyed or that the notary public does not possess the journal and does not know who possesses it or where it is located; and

5) A statement that, if the notary public subsequently acquires possession of the lost or stolen journal, the notary public shall file a written statement with the Secretary of State within 10 business days after the date the notary public reacquires possession of the lost or stolen journal, including a written explanation of how the journal was recovered.

(Source: Added at 47 Ill. Reg. 8640, effective June 5, 2023)

Section 176.950 Inspection of a Journal, Response to Subpoenas and Investigative Requests, and Public Information

a) In the notary's presence, any person may inspect an entry in the official journal of notarial acts during the notary's regular business hours, but only if:

1) The person's identity is personally known to the notary or proven through satisfactory evidence;

2) The person affixes a signature in the journal in a separate, dated entry;

3) The person specifies the month, year, type of document, and the name of the principal for the notarial act or acts sought; and

4) The person is shown only the entry or entries specified.

b) If the notary has a reasonable and explainable belief that a person has a criminal or harmful intent in requesting information from the notary's journal, the notary may deny access to any entry or entries.

c) Subpoenas and investigative requests. A request for inspection or certified copies of a journal made through an investigative request by law enforcement or by the

Secretary of State or in a subpoena in the course of criminal or civil litigation, or administrative proceeding shall be complied with in the manner specified in the request or subpoena.

d) If any portion of the audio-video recording of an electronic or remote notarization includes biometric information or includes an image of the identification card used to identify the principal, that portion of the recording is confidential and shall not be released without consent of the individual whose identity is being established, unless ordered by a court of competent jurisdiction or upon request by the Secretary of State.

e) Failure of a notary public to promptly and adequately respond to a request for public information in accordance with this Part may be good cause for suspension or revocation of a notary public or electronic notary public commission or other disciplinary action against the notary.

(Source: Added at 47 Ill. Reg. 8640, effective June 5, 2023)

Section 176.960 Electronic Journal Record Retention and Depositories

a) A notary public must retain the electronic journal required and any audio-video recording created under 5 ILCS 312/6A-104 in a computer or other electronic storage device that protects the journal and recording against unauthorized access by password or cryptographic process. The recording must be created in an industry-standard, audio-visual file format and must not include images of any electronic record that was the subject of the electronic or remote notarization.

b) An electronic journal must be retained for at least 7 years after the last electronic or remote notarial act chronicled in the journal. An audio-visual recording must be retained for at least 7 years after the recording is made.

c) A notary public must take reasonable steps to ensure that a backup of the electronic journal and audio-visual recording exists and is secure from unauthorized use.

d) Upon the death or adjudication of incompetency of a current or former notary public, the notary public's personal representative or guardian or any other person knowingly in possession of an electronic journal or audio-visual recording must:

1) Comply with the retention requirements of this Section;

2) Transmit the journal and recording to one or more depositories under subsection (e); or

3) Transmit the journal and recording in an industry-standard readable data storage device to the Illinois Secretary of State, Index Department at 111 E. Monroe St., Springfield, IL 62756.

e) A notary public, guardian, conservator, or agent of a notary public, or a personal representative of a deceased notary public may, by written contract, engage a third person to act as a depository to provide the storage required by this Section. A third person under contract under this Section shall be considered a depository.

The contract must:

1) Enable the notary public, guardian, conservator, or agent of the notary public, or the personal representative of the deceased notary public to comply with the retention requirements of this Section even if the contract is terminated; or

2) Provide that the information will be transferred to the notary public, guardian, conservator, or agent of the notary public, or the personal representative of the deceased notary public if the contract is terminated.

f) The retention requirements for this Part do not apply to notaries in the course of their employment with a governmental entity.

(Source: Added at 47 Ill. Reg. 8640, effective June 5, 2023)

Section 176.980 Revocation, Suspension, and Reprimand

For purposes of this Section, "notary public" includes an electronic notary public and remote notary public.

a) Revocation. A notary public's commission may be revoked for any of the foregoing acts or omissions:

1) The notary public demonstrates the notary public lacks the honesty, integrity, competence, or reliability to act as a notary public; or

2) The notary public fails to maintain a residence or place of employment in Illinois.

b) Suspension. A notary public's commission may be suspended for any actions contrary to the Act, other laws of the State of Illinois, and this Part.

c) Other Remedial Actions. The Secretary of State may deliver a written official warning to cease misconduct, misfeasance, or malfeasance to any notary public whose actions are determined to violate this Part, the Act, or other laws of the State of Illinois.

d) Before suspending or revoking a notary public's commission, the Secretary of State must inform the notary public of the basis for the suspension or revocation and that the suspension or revocation takes effect on a particular date unless a request for an administrative hearing is filed with the Secretary of State under 5 ILCS 312/7-108(j) and Section 176.990 before that date.

e) Resignation or expiration of a notary public's commission does not terminate or preclude an inquiry into the notary's conduct by the Secretary of State. Whether the finding would have been grounds for revocation will be made a matter of public record.

(Source: Added at 47 Ill. Reg. 8640, effective June 5, 2023)

Section 176.990 Appeals

Appeals should be addressed to the Secretary of State Department of Administrative Hearings and comply with Subpart K.

(Source: Added at 47 Ill. Reg. 8640, effective June 5, 2023) ∎

About the NNA

Since 1957, the National Notary Association has been committed to serving and educating the nation's Notaries. During that time, the NNA° has become known as the most trusted source of information for and about Notaries and Notary laws, rules and best practices.

The NNA serves Notaries through its NationalNotary.org website, social media, publications, annual conferences, seminars, online training and the NNA° Hotline, which offers immediate answers to specific questions about notarization.

In addition, the NNA offers the highest quality professional supplies, including official seals and stamps, recordkeeping journals, Notary certificates and Notary bonds.

Though dedicated primarily to educating and assisting Notaries, the NNA supports implementing effective Notary laws and informing the public about the Notary's vital role in today's society.

To learn more about the National Notary Association, visit NationalNotary.org. ■

Index